Elements of
Alternate Style

Elements of Alternate Style

. . . .

essays on writing and revision

. . . .

edited by **W**ENDY **B**ISHOP

Boynton/Cook Publishers
Heinemann
Portsmouth, NH

Boynton/Cook Publishers, Inc.
A subsidiary of Reed Elsevier Inc.
361 Hanover Street
Portsmouth, NH 03801-3912
Offices and agents throughout the world

Elements of alternate style : essays on writing and revision / edited
    by Wendy Bishop.
        p.   cm.
    ISBN: 0-86709-423-0 (acid-free paper)
    1. English language—Rhetoric—Study and teaching. 2. English
language—Rhetoric. 3. English language—Style. 4. Editing.
I. Bishop, Wendy.
PE1404.E44 1997
808'.042'07—dc21   97-3435
                                                                                        CIP

Editor: Peter R. Stillman
Cover Design: Renée M. Nicholls
Manufacturing: Louise Richardson

Printed in the United States of America on acid-free paper
00 99 98 97 DA   1 2 3 4 5 6

Contents

I

Invitations to Alternate Styles

Alternate Styles for Who, What, and Why? Some Introductions to *Elements of Alternate Style: Essays on Writing and Revision* (Including an E-Mail Interview with Winston Weathers)

A Story

Yesterday, I helped my eight-year-old son with his homework for third grade by being an admiring audience (who says writers write alone?). He prepared to undertake the following task: "Write a paragraph about special memories," and he began with the sentence "If I ever left [home], I would have a lot of memories like the house and the pool."

He stopped and thought a while, and I dreaded the next question—expecting "What should I write now?"—because it would lead me to a (teacher's) response that I didn't particularly want to make: "Why don't you add more details?" However, the result of his silence was the more astonishing offer to be *done*.

He said: "You can have paragraphs of just one sentence."

"Yes you can," I said, knowing that's not what his teacher expected for an assigned paragraph writing but glad he was raising the issue.

"I know," he said, "from my books—when someone's talking, like 'he said,' 'she said,' that's one sentence and that's one paragraph."

"Yes," I said, impressed that he was drawing style points from his reading.

"But can I start a sentence with *but*," he asked next.

And we went on.

A Quotation

From Winston Weathers, a teacher of writing whose ideas on writing in alternate styles have influenced many of the contributors in this book:

> So we (perversely?) teach "the composition." We do not teach form at all. We teach "a form" or at best a little bevy of closely related forms—"report," "personal essay," "article," "paper." All cousins. We do not teach form as a principle, but as a thing. We do not teach form as a process, but as an object. We do not teach form as an experience, but as a shape. And "shape" itself in a very limited sense: a shape that will fit the square hole already prepared for it in our little heads. ("Taxis/And the Teaching of English" 17)

3

A Response

A group of writers who are also writing teachers gathers together and decides to teach compositions, plural, to teach unrelated and related forms, to seek out distant cousins, black sheep and adopted relatives, and to valorize form as a process, form as experience, form as many shapes, form as the activity that enlarges the options of our minds. What they produce are the fifteen essays in this collection that seek not to replace what you know about writing, what you've learned so far, but to augment, complicate, tease, challenge, and extend what you do as a writer.

An (E-Mail) Interview

WB: Could you tell some stories about what prompted you to become involved in issues of style?

WW: All my life I've been arranging words on paper. (Now on the computer monitor.) Have always thought of composition (whatever kind) as con-struction work. How do we put the bricks together? Can we find new building materials? What does the final product look like? I've always enjoyed taking a piece of writing apart (in the laboratory, that is) to see what makes it "tick," "hold together." I see "writings" much as I see "'build-ings." What is the architecture? What is the style? I'm less concerned, as a writer/teacher, with content—heretical as that may sound—than with form, texture, configuration. Of course, there's the fun of matching content and form. A "building" should be appropriate for the "business" that it houses. But a good writer—like a good architect—should know how to design and build all kinds of structures: traditional, art deco, baroque, functional, etc. Who knows what "content" requirements will be presented to us day after day? A concern with style is a concern with being prepared to build the best composition we can whatever the content happens to be.

   [As a writing teacher] I didn't think it was my job to teach the students what to say or even how to think. I was only a few years older than the students themselves. But I could certainly teach them about words, language, writing. As for *An Alternate Style: Options in Composition*, it evolved quite simply. I'd long noticed that much of the great literature I was teaching was not written in the traditional straight/linear mode. I'd noticed, too, that out in the "real world," a great many of the messages presented in advertising, publicity, promotion, in personal letters, journals, diaries, and even in more daring book reviews, testimonials, meditations, etc. were using writing techniques that no one in the nation's English departments seemed to be teaching. The Academy occasionally acknowledged the existence of "experimental writing" but never suggested that ordinary writers might also practice something like it. My goal in writing *An Alternate Style* was simply to say to students (and their teachers) that there's more to writing than the style usually found in the Freshman theme, the second-semester research report, or the graduate literary essay.

WB: Could you share some of your responses as you flip through the essays of this book—*Elements of Alternate Style: Essays on Writing and Revision*—informal, associational, critical, anecdotal? We're interested in your impressions of this work derived from your work (in some cases) or work that took these authors to what I think are similar places, though perhaps by different paths.

WW: I believe these invigorating essays will contribute to a better understanding of the writing process in general and the stylistic options that every serious writer needs in her/his writing "wardrobe." Each of us writes for so many different reasons in this complicated world of ours that we need a lot of flexibility and diversity in our collection of writing skills and styles. These essays will encourage anyone who teaches writing to open some doors and windows and let fresh air and light into the classroom, not to displace the "basics" or "Grammar A," but rather to enlarge our definition of "good writing" so that our students can more effectively communicate with their fellow human beings.

Responding to the individual contributions: I much enjoyed the fast-food metaphor that Darrell Fike and Devan Cook present in the opening essay. I agree. Who wants the same hamburger served the same way every time we eat out? Most of us enjoy switching to pizza and even tacos, now and then. Nor do we need to stop there. A really sophisticated "eater" may reach out for something beyond fast food itself, maybe something gourmet, perhaps even champagne and caviar on occasion.

A number of the essays present interesting, even provocative things to do in the classroom, showing us, as Ronald A. DePeter does, how to use "found materials" and to create "fractured narratives." (A teacher may need, of course, to define "found material" very carefully to help students avoid unacceptable borrowings from copyrighted texts.) And Elsie Rogers, in what she calls "warming-up exercises," shows how to encourage creativity and invention by placing extraordinary restraints upon the writing task: write only in monosyllabic words, for instance. One might, additionally, ask students to write only in polysyllabic or Greco-Latinate words. Or one might ask students to transform an essay into a poem, the poem into a story, the story back into an essay. (I especially like Rogers' doing "the exercise . . . in class with my students." I've always believed that a teacher should be able and willing to do anything the student is asked to do, even if what the teacher creates isn't particularly brilliant. There's nothing wrong with showing students that even a teacher can have a bad day, write "blah" material, make a fool of himself/herself.)

Lad Tobin, by wrestling with the problem of teaching Grammar A and Grammar B side by side, strengthens the argument for using Grammar B in our teaching and shows how one Grammar B device, "double voice," has been widely and acceptably used in a lot of pedestrian places as well as in literature. Tobin's defense of Grammar B is matched by Amy Cashulette Flagg's interesting approach to the research paper: enlarging the definition of research itself and showing us how Grammar-B thinking can wipe away some of the mold and dust from the paper as it is usually taught. Kim Haimes Korn throws new light, also, upon the necessary and well established writing act of revision.

Both Elizabeth Rankin and Hans Ostrom rejoice in the "fun and entertainment" aspect of Grammar B, and heaven knows we need some fun and entertainment in the classroom once in awhile—though I suppose the most obligatory focus for a writer is upon the audience, not upon the self. But if one can do right by the reader and at the same time have fun in the writing, so much the better.

In a theory-rich essay, Nancy Reichert, via her own journal entries, presents an intriguing way to help students discover their own boundaries and parameters as far as audience and subject matter are concerned. Though I think a few taboos are helpful for all of us, it certainly doesn't hurt to identify them before we sally forth to express ourselves. Reichert makes use of a grid to explain her classroom research, and liking grids myself, I would propose the following one for teachers of writing to suggest the range of styles we all need to know about, master, and demonstrate for our students.

Writing Styles

Energy	Grammar A			Grammar B	
	Low	*Medium*	*High*	*Lite*	*Heavy*
Formal	X	X	X	X	X
Informal	X	X	X	X	X
Colloq.	X	X	X	X	X

The nine profiles of Grammar A take into consideration not only the conventional writing levels but also the degree of energy to be found in a style. As for Grammar B, I now use the terms "lite" and "heavy" to suggest just how differentiated from Grammar A we want our alternate/alternative style to be. Sometimes we want to use Grammar B to enliven a composition that is, appropriately, written in Grammar A. Other times, though, we need a more vigorously differentiated style in order to say things that Grammar A can't quite get said.

Which leads me to Thomas O'Donnell's thoughtful essay in which he wisely points out that both Grammar A and Grammar B, comprising as they both do all sorts of well-known speech acts, "emerge as attempts to act on readers in certain ways—they serve rhetorical ends and purposes." He argues that most of our students already know a great deal about communicating and, if I read him right, our task as teachers is primarily to guide and direct students into an increasingly effective use of what they already know. O'Donnell says, "I don't like being a correctness cop," and I wholeheartedly agree. One way out of that uncomfortable role, I think, is to leave the world of "errors" altogether. When a student writes "between you and I," I'd prefer to put a circle around it and ask the student why he/she chose to do that. Was it for some purpose? How do you think your reader will feel about it? This "taboo" use of the nominative case probably won't work for your grammarian uncle or your history professor; in a personal letter the absence of the objective case may be O.K. If a student writes "accomodate," I ask why that spelling was chosen. For what purpose? To be funny? To look uneducated? To irritate some prescriptive-minded reader? If the writer says there was no particular purpose, I point out that there's the error, the lack of insight into what is being done. And I'd have the writer review the spellings: "accommodate," the usual Grammar A dictionary spelling; "accomodate," the popular spelling used by over fifty percent of Americans; "akomodate," the phonetic spelling that might be used for very special literary purposes. And I'd point out to all my students that we don't, if we're truly educated, try to decide in advance on the correctness of "It is I," "It is me," "It's I," or "It's me." We're prepared to write/say any of them. Appropriateness, not "correctness," will determine our selection.

Finally, I agree with Michael Spooner's call for an "ethics of editing." Having been grievously edited at times by well meaning but uninformed editors, I know what it feels like, as a writer, to see one's meanings and intentions destroyed by an editorial imposition of "consistency and correctness" upon any and every text that comes along. And I'm sure students must feel the same way when everything they write is edited/corrected back into a narrow version of Grammar A (the "plain style," for instance). Of course, Grammar B does present editing problems, but careful consultation with the author will nearly always discover what's deliberate and what isn't deliberate, what works and what doesn't work, and what needs changing and what should be left alone.

Wendy Bishop, in her own essay, takes us back to the sine qua non of all our writing, the English sentence, showing us that the sentence is not something "cut and dried" but is a beautifully versatile language act. Going through her own house, picking up all the different kinds of texts she can find there, the real-life texts with which human beings live every day, she reads and analyzes in order to learn to write—for it is from the full range of writing, from textbooks to magazine ads, from love letters to curricula vitae, from poem to annual report that all our grammars derive, Grammar A and Grammar B, and whatever other grammars are out there for us to identify and emulate. By bringing these essays together and by writing an essay herself, Bishop nudges us forward into a larger pedagogical space, encouraging teachers to start "asking, how—how did the writer" put her/ his words together to reach a particular readership on a particular occasion.

I'm glad this collection of essays has been put together. It covers essential aspects of both writing and the teaching of writing. The essays talk about writing, especially some of the newly discovered frontiers of writing, and at the same time demonstrate, in a variety of ways, the principle that they are addressing (and here I happily include, too, essays by Alys Culhane, Carrie Leverenz, and Ruth Mirtz, each offering other alternate visions).

I find in this collection of essays, devoted to "elements of alternate style," a wonderful enthusiasm for and about the English language and its many styles and grammars. And as we all know, it is only with enthusiasm that we keep our work as teachers and writers alive.

The Traditional Editor's Introduction and Exhortation to Readers

This book is intended for writers and teachers of writing. I hope you might, as a writer, sit down and read it for the ways it can help you—reminding you of what you already know, encouraging you to go to new places. For a teacher, I hope these essays and the spirit of the book provide you with support for teaching writing the way you know it should be taught.

Outside of classrooms, *Elements of Alternate Style* should be an alternate reference tool much as the stylebooks I have played off of for this book's title. In the classroom, I trust it will provide discussion points and exercises. It should stoke enthusiasm and raise some dissent for the history of style and writing instruction has never been without strong opinions.

Part One consists of an introduction and six essays that could structure an initial classroom sequence—asking writers to try writing exercises and to reconsider how they have constructed essays in the past, how they might construct them today by looking and looking again, by fracturing and creating double voices, by reconsidering the place of research. Part Two consists of five essays that push these explorations further. The authors here argue that writing IS about taking risks, trying (sometimes failing), and learning from exploration, from play, from taking radical twists and turns. Of course, writers and teachers of writers who follow this path have to allow for risk by rewarding it, have to encourage failure-as-learning by exploring the processes of learning about styles by trying them on (some teaching and learning ideas in the appendix support this attitude). Part Three raises broader issues of writers' identities, technology, correctness, and editing as authors share their experiences in these areas.

Read sequentially, the essays in *Elements of Alternate Style* will encourage you to loosen up a bit as a stylist, then encourage you to take wing, to wing it, to push the envelope of "safe writing" as it is commonly defined, and the final essays will encourage you to enter writers' discussions about style. But just as we don't write from A to G to T to Z, you don't have to read these essays from A to Z, either. Books are linear, thinking is not. I encourage you to read like a writer, entering these conversations about style at any convenient and enticing entry point.

Thank Yous

To the many fine writing students and writing teachers at Florida State University, some still here, some gone to other places, whose work informs and is part of this book. To the contributors to this book who worked with humor, energy and dedication to revise and revise and revise, to risk and risk and risk. To Peter Stillman who always shares his friendship and lends dependable editorial support. To Boynton/Cook Heinemann editorial and production staffs who help willingly and well. To Winston Weathers for sharing his time, memories, enthusiasm and skill in ways that helped me build a better book. To Morgan, and Tait. Yes, particularly to Morgan and Tait, who always like to see their names once, twice.

Works Cited

Weathers, Winston. 1980. *An Alternate Style: Options in Composition*. Rochelle Park, NJ: Hayden Book Company.

[A Portion of this book was originally published in *Freshman English News*, Winter, 1976, under the title "The Grammars of Style: New Options in Composition" and then reprinted as "The Grammars of Style: New Options in Composition" in *Rhetoric and Composition: A Sourcebook for Teachers and Writers*. 3rd ed. Ed. Richard L. Graves. 1990. Portsmouth, NH: Boynton/Cook Heinemann, 200–214. Unfortunately, the original book, *An Alternate Style*, is out of print at this time.]

Weathers, Winston. Summer 1980. "Taxis/And the Teaching of English." *Journal of English Teaching Techniques* 15–20.

1

"Would You Like Fries with That?"
Ordering Up Some Writing: Fast Food for Thought

Darrell Fike and Devan Cook

Would You Like Fries with That?

Lunch time. You go to your favorite fast-food place. It doesn't matter which one you go to—this one, the one across town, the one in China. Everything is the same. Quick, easy, neat. Line up and place your order.

The clerk smiles and asks, "Would you like fries with that?"

Behind the counter, the uniforms scurry to the bins with bag in hand. On the wall hangs a row of plastic pictures of the food. A little chart diagrams your order's preparation and presentation. It doesn't matter which one you go to— this one, the one across town, the one in China. Everything is the same. Quick, easy, neat. The only difference is how many of each in this bag or that.

You pay and take your food. You nibble on a fry as you walk away. Soon the bag is emptied and your stomach is full. You wad up the bag, crush your drink cup, and throw them away. Quick, easy, neat. Later someone asks what you had for lunch. You can't remember.

All around the world in a thousand places just like this one a clerk is asking a customer, "Would you like fries with that?"

Everything is the same.

would you like fries with that   small, medium, or large   for here or to go   no substitutions allowed   your total comes to   drive thru to the cashier window may I take your order   would you like fries with that

Ordering Up Some Writing

English class. You take out your notebook and uncap your favorite pen. It doesn't matter what you write about—yourself, someone you don't know, or the topic the teacher wrote on the board. Everything is the same. Fill up the page with words. Follow the rules.

The teacher smiles and says, "Write."

In every row, students bend over their desks and begin. In your textbook are lists of rules for good writing. You follow the rules you remember. It doesn't matter what you write about—yourself, someone you don't know, or the topic the teacher wrote on the board. Everything is the same. Fill up the page with words. Follow the rules.

Sometimes you want to break the rules. Write the way that sounds best to you. A way that makes your writing fun and different. But you know better. Some writing is right, and some writing is wrong. The book says so.

You finish writing. You make sure all your sentences are complete and all your paragraphs have topic sentences. You put your name on your essay and pass it forward. Later someone asks you what you wrote about. You can't remember.

All around the world in a thousand classrooms just like this one a teacher is telling the students, "Write."

Everything is the same.

be sure to follow the rules   don't repeat words   don't use incomplete sentences   express a single main idea   develop each paragraph fully provide adequate transitions, a conclusion   be sure to follow the rules

Fast Food for Thought

Not all writing has to be the same. Sometimes you need to break the rules. Not just to break them but for a reason—your purpose demands that you do. Many professional writers break the rules to make their writing interesting or to help them say what they mean.

As tasty and filling as burgers are, you don't always want one for lunch.

Sometimes you crave something different, say like a pizza. Pizza, though it does offer the possibility of new and different combinations of toppings, is basically meat and bread like a burger, only rearranged. But pizza sure seems different—and tasty—when you are burned out on burgers.

Trying a new style of writing can be a nice change, too. You still use the same words and punctuation as before, only in a fresh way. By trying a different style you may not only make your writing more interesting and tasty, you may also discover new ideas hiding behind the rules you bend or break.

Winston Weathers, a writing specialist, calls breaking the rules an alternate "grammar of style." Not a bad or wrong grammar, just one that is different. By grammar of style, Weathers means the "set of conventions governing the construction of the whole composition" (200–201). The traditional grammar of style, the one we are usually taught in school, builds upon a sense of order and consistency. Essays must contain an introduction with a thesis, a body that develops supporting points in logical sequence, and a conclusion that sums up the main ideas. Sentences must be complete and must link together in an unbroken chain.

While the traditional grammar of style is okay for some topics and essays, Weathers feels that students should be told about alternate grammars of style to give them more options when writing. He says this alternate grammar of style is used successfully by professional writers and is simply another tool for student writers to use in expressing their ideas:

> It is an alternate grammar, no longer an experiment, but a mature grammar used by competent writers and offering students of writing a well-tested "set of options" that, added to the traditional grammar of style, will give them a much more flexible voice, a much greater opportunity to put into effective language all the things they have to say. (202-203)

Have It Your Way

Let's talk about some of Weathers' ideas. Only we are going to turn them into food. Fast food is good sometimes—quick, easy, neat—but we like two foods that let us participate in creating what we eat: pizza and salad.

So if you're hungry for ideas about alternate styles (or if your teacher is making you read this essay), read on. If you're just plain hungry, go get something to eat.

Writing a Pizza

Pizza is a nice balance between the required and the optional. You need a good crust and toppings, for sure. But what kind of crust, round or square, thin or thick, crispy or chewy, is up to you. So are the toppings—the choices are limited only by your imagination and the endurance of your taste buds. Weathers has some options for alternate styles that will help you write a pizza.

By the Slice. Weathers calls this technique writing with "crots." Think of how a pizza is cut into slices—you can pull out one and enjoy it by itself. All together the slices make the whole pizza.

A crot is an "autonomous unit, characterized by the absence of any transitional devices that might relate it to the preceding or subsequent crots" (203).

Crots are sections, or slices, of writing that are assembled to create an essay. Crots can be a single sentence, like a proverb or fortune cookie saying, or they can be as long as a whole page. Leave some blank space between them, stack them up and down the page, or put them side by side. Sometimes they are numbered.

So write a pizza: Don't focus on transitions or making each paragraph lead right into the next one. Let the reader make the connections for herself, melt the ideas together in her mind.

You just make sure each slice is tasty.

Free Sample: Crots

Notice how part of the first page could be redone using crots:
Not all writing has to be the same.
Quick, easy, neat.
Behind the counter, the uniforms scurry to the bins with bag in hand. On the wall hangs a row of plastic pictures of the food. A little chart diagrams your order's preparation and presentation.
You pay and take your food. You nibble on a fry as you walk away.
Quick, easy, neat.

Listing. Weathers says you might want to make a list in your essay. He says a list usually "contains a minimum of five items, the items being related in subject matter and presented in list form to avoid indicating any other relationships among the items than that they are there all at once, that they are parts of a whole" (206).

Think of how the toppings for a pizza are listed: pepperoni, mushrooms, sausage, peppers, onions, olives, anchovies, bacon, pineapple. The only relationship among them is that they can go on a pizza. In your essay, make a list of the characteristics of whatever you are talking about. Don't comment on the list. Let the reader fill in the connections. Weathers says that when a writer uses a list he or she is "simply giving you the data, the evidence, the facts, the object" and that "the reader must add them up and evaluate them" (207).

Free Sample: Listing

If you were making a list for an essay about pizza, you might start with a whole sentence or two and then make a list:
Pizza is one of my favorite meals.
thin crust, thick crust
stringy melting cheese
saving some for later
picking off the pepperoni
who gets the last slice
waiting for the delivery

We have listed phrases, but you could list single words or longer phrases, depending on what works best for your ideas and your essay.

Mouth Stuffer or a Nibble. Weathers identifies two kinds of nontraditional sentences that professional writers use: the labyrinthine sentence (from labyrinth or maze) and the sentence fragment. Traditional styles tell us not to use these types of sentences, but Weathers says they can be very effective if used purposefully and with care.

Sometimes when eating pizza you take a great big bite—a mouth stuffer—filling your mouth up and maybe getting a little sauce and cheese on your chin. This is what the labyrinthine sentence is like.

Sometimes you take just a nibble of the end or pick off a favorite bit of topping. This is what the sentence fragment is like.

The labyrinthine sentence is a long sentence that keeps going and going and going. Weathers says that this kind of sentence can replicate the complexity and confusion of a situation. The reader—if you take care that he or she doesn't get confused by all the twists and turns in your labyrinth—moves along quickly like on a roller-coaster ride. Be careful, though, sometimes too big of a bite can make it hard to chew!

A sentence fragment is a piece of sentence broken off for emphasis, often only a single word or a short phrase. Weathers says that this little nibble of a sentence draws attention to itself and can suggest fragmentation and isolation. Fragments also are effective when used to contrast or balance traditional sentences or the labyrinthine sentence. Be careful, though, because just like you wouldn't want to nibble your way through a whole pizza, you don't want to overuse the sentence fragment in an essay.

Save it for when it really counts, like the last piece of pepperoni you pick off the pizza before you finish it.

Free Sample: Labyrinthine and Sentence Fragments

Here is a labyrinthine sentence about making a birthday cake:

It's good but not what I set out to do, like the banana birthday cake I baked, iced, cooled, Tupperware-d, and dropped on the kitchen floor on my way to the party so it stayed clean in its container but broke into huge moist chunks jagged as broken rocks or icebergs, to be rescued by folding in nuts and crumbs into whipped sour cream, and served sliced from a star-shaped mold—tasted okay, but an inhospitable environment for candles.

Here is part of this sentence rewritten using fragments:

. . . stayed clean in its container. But broke into huge moist chunks. Jagged as broken rocks or icebergs.

Two for One Coupon. So when we use these elements of alternate style to write a pizza—crots, listing, labyrinthine sentences, and fragments—we are allowing the reader to join with us in the fun.

Like inviting a friend along to use your two-for-one coupon.

Writing a Salad

Salads are versatile: you can mix and match most anything you like and make a salad. Salads are a little more diverse and jumbled than pizza.

Sometimes in a salad you want ingredients that contrast each other or seem like an odd combination. Weathers has some ideas we think work great to help you write a salad.

Tossing a Salad. Weathers calls this "collage/montage."

Collage/montage writing is when "diverse elements are patched together to make the whole composition" (213). Lines of poetry, descriptions, dialogue, headlines, regular writing, and even drawings are put together like a collage to create an essay. Think of collages you have seen or maybe done for school. All the different cut-outs, drawings, and words appear separately but come together to create a unified effect. Same with the collage/montage essay.

Like making a salad at the salad bar: you put in your favorite stuff and toss it all around. A little of this and a little of that. When you're done you have a big, beautiful, one-of-a-kind salad on your plate.

Free Sample: Collage Montage

You might like to try cutting and pasting to help create your collage/montage, or use different styles of writing or typefaces. Remember: writing, like salad making, involves movement:

My cousin Bill rode from Riyadh in Saudi Arabia to Amman, Jordan, on a camel. His only supplies: tea and bread, coffee and dates. Fuel to cross a thousand miles of desert.

Coffee is one of the first necessities of life. Larousse Gastronomique

FLYING SAUCER SEARCHING FOR MISSING CUP LANDS ON WHITE HOUSE LAWN

"Iced coffee?? Double gag!!"

Turkish coffee: cardamom, mint, sugar, sludgy coffee grounds in the bottom of small china cup: delta mud.

Instant. *Fresh ground.* Percolate. *Drip.* Steam. *Cream and sugar. Black.* Au lait. *Con leche.* Java. Cup of Joe. *Expresso.* Wide awake now.

A Second Helping. Weathers says that repeating yourself is okay, if it is done for a good reason. For a good reason. Not just to take up room or add words. Repeating a word, a phrase, or a sentence can energize your essay giving it feeling of movement and momentum. Repeating a word, a phrase, or a sentence can replicate the sameness of an experience or provide a feeling of finality or inevitability.

Standing at the salad bar, you add one more scoop of croutons to your salad, another spoon of pineapple chunks, another tong full of cucumber slices. Repeating the important elements gives your salad the zest and appeal you want it to have. Emphasizes your love of garbanzo beans or sliced mushrooms.

But be careful: if you put too much of one item—repeat it unnecessarily—you won't have room on your plate for something new!!

Free Sample: Repetition

At the beginning of our essay, we used repetition in both the fast food and classroom scenes. Look for repeated phrases or words. Read them again.

Mix and Match. Weathers says that professional writers sometimes use a technique he calls "double-voice." This technique takes different forms—regular type contrasted with italic, information mixed-in with questions and comments about the information, or even two columns of text running parallel to each other with each talking about different aspects of the subject or even different subjects.

Writers use this alternate style when "they feel that they could say this *or* that about a subject; when they feel that two attitudes toward a subject are equally valid; when they wish to suggest two sides to the story . . . or when they wish to effect a style 'corresponding' to ambiguous realities" (208).

Like with a salad. Sometimes you add something different to contrast the other flavors. Like adding raisins to go with the onions or mixing bleu cheese and honey mustard dressing.

Too many voices, like too many ingredients, can turn your essay, like a salad, into a gloppy mess. So use double-voice with care and only when you really need to.

Free Sample: Double-Voice

We often talk to ourselves—do you? Sometimes we "think out loud" as we move down the salad bar filling up our plates. Try thinking out loud in your essay by using double-voice to answer a question you've asked or to make a comment from another point of view.

lettuce	healthy stuff
spinach	low-cal, Vitamin A
green peppers	**jalapenos**
grated carrots	
cauliflower	
broccoli	Where's the rabbit?
beets	Good Grief!!
cottage cheese	now some cheddar
	bacon bits
	croutons
	lots of croutons—green glares!
oil and vinegar	bleu cheese
	more bleu cheese

Writing is like making a salad—start with a clean plate.

Good and Good for You. So when we use these elements of alternate style—collage, repetition, double-voice—we are mixing up our essay a little to make it better.

Just like with a salad.

Too Much of Good Thing

Richard Hugo, a well regarded poet and writing teacher, encourages writers to be experimental but also says that you have to be careful when using an alternate style: "That is the advantage of making up rules. If they are working, they should lead you to better writing. If they don't, you've made up the wrong rules" (43).

So keep experimenting until you put together a style that works best for you. Start with the traditional style and make a few changes here and there. Try out some of the ideas that we have talked about. Like trying a new topping on a pizza or a different dressing on your salad.

You just might like it.

Works Cited

Hugo, Richard. 1979. *The Triggering Town.* New York: Norton.

Weathers, Winston. 1990. "The Grammars of Style: New Options in Composition." *Rhetoric and Composition: A Sourcebook for Teachers and Writers.* 3rd ed. Ed. Richard L. Graves. Portsmouth, NH: Boynton/Cook Heinemann. 200–214.

2

Stretch a Little and Get Limber
Warming up to (and With) Grammar B

Elsie Rogers

Grammar is a piano I play by ear, since I seem to have been out of
school the year the rules were mentioned.

Joan Didion, "Why I Write"

"Okay class! It's exercise time! Get out your pad and pen. We're going to write
for about ten minutes. Be prepared to read what you write aloud," I say:

Write a half-page paragraph. Use only one-syllable words in this paragraph.
Your sentences should range from one word to ten words in length. (Adapted
from Hickey, 31–32)

"What do we write about?"
"Anything you want to. It's your choice."
"I can't write a whole paragraph using words with one syllable."
"Sure you can, just get started."
"It sounds stupid."
"Yeah, I know, but just try to do it. We'll talk about it when you finish."
After much laughing, counting of syllables, and asking out loud if a word
is one syllable or two, everyone finishes writing.
"Okay, get in your groups, read your paragraphs aloud, then discuss the

exercise. Was it difficult? Why? What were you able to write with the rules that
I gave you? What choices did the exercises force you to make?"

After about twenty minutes of moving from group to group, listening in on
their conversations, I say:

"It's time to get into a circle and share your findings."

Amy raises her hand and reads:

The Blue Bird

I saw a blue bird. It had blue wings. I watched it soar in the sky. Oh! so high.
I wish I could fly, so high. It would be fun to fly. My arms would be strong.
I would not be late to a date. I would fly fast like the blue bird. The blue bird
flew to the nest in the tree. In the nest were small blue birds. The small ones
said it was time to eat. The bird blue bird gave them a worm. I left. It was time
for me to walk home. I wish I could fly. Oh! so high, like the blue bird. Or
like the man in blue tights.

This exercise takes students back to "Dick and Jane" books, those first-
grade primers, back to a playful time. A time they created ghost runners when
there weren't enough players for two teams. When the tree by the house was
first base, and when any ball that went into the street was a foul ball and over
the neighbor's fence was a homerun.

When we originally wrote the one-syllable word paragraphs, we thought
in terms of simple topics and of simple use of language. But, after the first
writing and discussion we learned this was not necessarily true. Warren explains what he wanted to do with the one-syllable word paragraph:

I immediately chose to write in a first person description that was harsh and
with active voice so it was better read aloud than on the page. I wanted . . .
the story as if it were written by an idiot . . . I wanted the reader to get the feel
for a simple-minded, vindictive fool who can't phrase his feelings well. (JE
9/5/95)

Warren accomplishes his goal of writing a paragraph that sounds good read
aloud:

She Has to Have Her Way

She's got to have it. I don't know why. I don't want to know why. All I know
is that she's a real sly girl. A child who can't make up her mind. First she
wants this then she wants that . . . Don't give in or let up or back down. If you
have to kill her, call it a good thing, then back off. But the truth comes out
once and for all. And I have to give up. I hate to give up. She makes me give
up. She makes them all give up. She has to have her way all her own. You just
can't fight it.

Warren created this paragraph within fifteen minutes and later in the same
class revised this paragraph into a story entitled, "The Ant Girl: She Has to
Have Her Way." Warren, also, drew a wonderful ink sketch of the Ant Girl on
the back of his story.

My students and I have been writing these in-class exercises for a couple of years now, but this semester we have done this particular one-syllable words exercise twice. Why do the same exercise twice? On the first try most students think they must write for first-grade readers. But, after the first writing and discussion, students see one-syllable words and short sentences as not necessarily simple, therefore, their second tries are more complex.

The following is Judith's second try at the one-syllable word exercise:

> The waves roll in as I watch my beach. My day did not have to start off this bad. 10:00 a.m., a tide from hell. Rough seas, kids tossed, boards lost. I hear a child scream and search for the source. With his arms thrown up, he went down. I leapt off the chair and off I ran. Oh God! Not now! Such a young boy. I dove in the sea and swam. I swam with all my might. I reach him, but out of breath. He had breath left in him. Not much though. I dragged the eight year old boy in. At the shore he was dead. I did C.P.R. for half an hour. Help came. The boy was dead. Such a young child, gone at age eight. Was it my fault? The courts said no . . . I say yes. I could have saved him.

After writing this paragraph, I asked students to revise the paragraphs they had just finished according to these new instructions. I say:

> Now I want you to revise those same paragraphs using these rules. Your sentences can range from one to eighteen words. This time you may use some two-syllable words but try to have at least half the words be only one syllable.
>
> Okay now, listen carefully to the last two instructions. Make each sentence four words shorter or four words longer than the sentence before it and make half of the sentences end in a consonant sound.
>
> Do I need to repeat these instructions? (Adapted from Hickey, 45)

Judith then reads her revision of the one-syllable paragraph according to these new rules:

> The waves came rolling in as I watched my stretch of the beach. My day didn't have to begin so badly. It was ten o'clock and last night's storm caused the worst possible tides. The seas were round and children were thrown about. When I heard the child's scream I peered out over the horizon for the source. His arms were flailing about as he went under. I leapt off my chair and began running towards the ocean. Oh God! Do you have to sacrifice this child. I dove in and began swimming as fast as possible. When I finally reached him I was out of breath. He was unconscious but not breathing. I brought him in, but by the time we reached the shore he was lifeless. Not a breath left in him. About sixteen minutes later he was declared dead. Was it my fault? The courts said no, but I can't help but think I was.

We began discussion with our initial reactions to both paragraphs. The class agreed the first paragraph created an emotional reaction, while the second paragraph filled in the missing information adding more visual details. But, why did we react differently? It was essentially the same story with the same facts, so why did the first paragraph make us *feel* more and the second paragraph make us *understand* more? This question led to talk of alliteration, repetition, and short and long sentences with regard to power positions in sentences.

When we write according to these guidelines, we have the opportunity to see clearly what happens when we write with short sentences and one-syllable words, because we are not looking at a five- to ten-page paper full of other rambling sentences. Since the next exercise calls for us to alternate long and short sentences, we learn what happens when we vary sentence lengths. Thus we learn to be more conscious of what we are doing when we write. We also become more aware of other writers' techniques as we read their writings.

The following excerpt from Amy's essay, "The Ugly Duckling," combines the use of one-syllable words with repetition.

> I was one of those "too" people that my oh-so-cool new classmates didn't accept. I was too tall, too smart, too willing to answer questions in class, my hair was too curly, and I was too heavy. I knew I couldn't do anything about being too smart so I worked on the too heavy. I wasn't obese, just about fifteen pounds too big. I started running with my dad every night and watching what I ate. Somewhere along the line I stopped doing it for the people that thought that I wasn't good enough and started doing it because it made me feel good and look good. I did loose that extra baggage; I was by no means a Miss Universe, but I looked pretty good.

Amy presented this paper to the class for a full class workshop and was happy with the positive feedback she received on the repetition of the "too." In conference Amy told me she got the idea for the repetition in her paper from Dick Gregory's essay, "Shame," that we read in class and from the in-class exercises. She pointed to a few sentences as she read,

> Pregnant people get strange tastes. I was pregnant with poverty. Pregnant with dirt and pregnant with smells that made people turn away, pregnant with cold and pregnant with shoes that were never bought for me, pregnant . . . . (Gregory, 456)

Through paying attention to our different options as writers, we read as writers interested in form and we learn how form is an integral part of content. As in Judith's revision of the paragraph on the drowning, we also learned that form changes content.

In my own writing, I became aware how form changes content while doing "The Fifteen Sentence Portrait" from Wendy Bishop's *Working Words*. The exercise asks you to picture in your mind a person you have strong feelings for and that you may like or dislike, that person may be living or dead, but it's important that you know/knew the person. After you pick the person, you write fifteen sentences about that person in a prescribed way and order. We did this as an in-class writing, I chose to write about my mother because I had never been able to write to her. Since I had to write in a prescribed way, I said things about Mother I would never have said otherwise. I now know I was too close to her to say something new. I had made up my mind about her and our relationship so every time I wrote about her the same sentiments came out. This exercise done in class with my students created a distance for me that I needed to be truly honest about her. I later revised the portrait making it into a poem. This personal experience convinced me exercises were a valuable way for writers to learn their craft.

The "warm-ups" are comparable to a singer's exercises with pitch and breath control. A pianist's finger exercises. An artist practicing different brush strokes. A ballerina warming up with the five positions. Why shouldn't a writer warm up so that when the opportunity arises for using a certain rhetorical move, she can consciously choose because she understands and knows its capabilities as well as hers?

What can be learned by using an exercise as constrained as writing with only one-syllable words? By using one-syllable words, students discover how many one-syllable words there are, and how powerful they can be especially when they end in hard consonants such as *under*, *child*, *dead*, and *fault* as in Judith's paragraph. By constraining language in this way, writers hear the rhythm and can feel the power of one-syllable words and shorter sentences. We also develop a playful attitude toward language and a repertoire of stylistic options.

Warm-ups help us examine language use and open our ears and eyes for possible revisions. They are not meant to be particularly wonderful pieces of writing, but just for us to see what would happen if we followed these rules, instead of writing in the style that comes most naturally to us. Since writers want the final product to be "good" many of us tend to write in the style in which we are most fluent. I have found I am more willing to experiment with style in small exercises rather than all of a sudden change the style of a piece of writing that I am invested in. In fact, experimentation promotes the idea that everything you write does *not* have to be "good" to be worthwhile. When I first began teaching, I tried to get my students to revise rather than edit their papers, and for the most part, they resisted. Why do writers resist changing their writing style?

Comfort level. Fear that papers won't be as good. Embarrassment in front of peers. Fear of making a bad grade. As a student in the writing program and a poet, I stayed with a style that felt comfortable. Like Joan Didion, I played grammar like a piano. However, my ear is not as well tuned as Didion's. So if I happen to have a spectacular essay, or even if just parts are good, it's an accident. I sometimes start an essay ten different times before I find a voice that sounds right. My different "starts" of essays develop my ability to hear what will work and serve as warm-ups for me. Often these different starts are five to ten pages with each new beginning a revision of the one before it. I learn from our in-class warm-ups because I benefit from all of our tries.

Many students don't revise (re-vision) their papers because they don't understand what teachers mean by revision. So I began giving in-class exercises, which would prepare them for revision. By revising in-class exercises, like those shared here, we learn together how different styles of writing about the same subject produces very different papers on the same topics. In this first-year writing class, we concentrated on language use so the exercises gave us a daily look at different techniques used in communication such as conversation, monologue, dialogue, first-person narrative, etc. We also strove for sharp descriptions through exercises that promoted use of the five senses. We discussed Grammar B at the same time we discussed Grammar A, learning both at the same time. Through this discussion we learned how to properly construct a fragment, a labyrinthine sentence, crots, etc. We also talked about the appropriate audience for each. Finally, we not only know how a writer affected us, but why and how they did it.

Professional writers often write about their everyday ritual of writing. But, I have been a writer who doesn't write every day so my ability to hear well is hampered by my lack of exercise. Usually, I write to find out what I think. What I feel. What I know. But, sometimes I don't want to know what I think, what I feel, or what I know. So, I don't write.

Since I want to improve my writing, and since I believe writing everyday is the best way to improve, I continue borrowing exercises from many books on writing. The exercises have made it easier for me to write daily because I am not so self-conscious about what I have to say. Studying Hemingway's, Faulkner's, Welty's, O'Conner's style and that of other literary writers helps, but when I try to mimic their writing with their words in front of me, I become tongue-tied. I am intimidated. I can't hear my own words. As a result of this experience I began with exercises that allow me to create my own style. As a result of my own struggle to improve as a writer, I decided to continue these writerly habits with my students.

Exercises are for writers. They create an opportunity to talk about voice and how our word choice and sentence structure produce different tones. The ones shared here are borrowed from Dona J. Hickey's book *Developing a Written Voice*. In addition, for writing descriptions, labyrinthine sentences, and poetry I use Wendy Bishop's *Working Words* and *Released Into Language*; plus other guided writings from Natalie Goldberg's *Writing Down the Bones*; Carol Burke and Molly Best Tinsley's *The Creative Process*; and Robin Behn and Chase Twichell's *The Practice of Poetry*.

But you don't have to use guide books to make up your own exercises just like you don't have to go to a gym to work out. Mostly the exercises focus my attention on what I want to work on at a particular time. Paying attention for me also means taking pictures of what I am writing about. I take pictures of the object from many angles. While looking through the lens of a camera you narrow your vision so you can see more than you can see when you look at the bigger picture.

Since I am a Southerner I often read Southern writers listening for the rhythms and nuances of the language, or I go to a local gathering place listening to speech patterns and other noises of the place. If I want to write about a certain place then I go there physically (if possible), or I read about that place to get the sight, smells, sound, and feel of it right. I construct exercises for me to do that force me to grow as a writer or supply information I need to write. So all you need to do to make up your own exercises is to analyze what you need to work on, then create a way to pay attention to those needs.

Through questioning boundaries in writing from the beginning of the semester, by playing with form, style, and constantly changing the rules, I believe we learn how to use the rules to our advantage and how to make up our own rules when necessary.

Works Cited

Behn, Robin and Chase Twichell. 1992. *The Practice of Poetry: Writing Exercises from Poets Who Teach.* New York, NY: HarperPerennial.

Bishop, Wendy. 1992. *Working Words: The Process of Creative Writing.* Mountain View, CA: Mayfield.

Bishop, Wendy. 1990. *Released into Language: Options for Teaching Creative Writing.* Urbana, IL: National Council of Teachers of English.

Burke, Carol and Milly Best Tinsley. 1993. *The Creative Process.* New York, NY: St. Martin's.

Goldberg, Natalie. 1986. *Writing Down the Bones: Freeing the Writer Within.* Boston, MA: Shambhala.

Gregory, Dick. 1993. "Shame." *Windows: Exploring Personal Values Through Reading and Writing.* New York, NY: HarperCollins. 455–458.

Hickey, Dona J. 1993. *Developing a Written Voice.* Mountain View, CA: Mayfield.

3

Fractured Narratives
Explorations in Style

Ronald A. DePeter

I used to think of the term *fractured* as broken, something that would mend or heal with time. As kids, my friends and I knew you couldn't become an astronaut if you had a broken bone and, even though we defied common safety sense by recklessly jumping from rickety tree houses and across wide, half-frozen streams, we always had the same initial concern when somebody fell or landed wrong. "Is it broken?" we'd whisper, standing over the victim as he moaned and rubbed his shin or elbow.

I've turned the standard definition of fractured on its head in order to view the "breaking" that happens in the writing samples below—the breaking of conventional expectations—less as a setback or limitation, or even something to be mended or fixed or changed, but a technique to be appreciated as a productive way of getting at new, unexplored relationships between writers and their texts and between writers and their readers.

I think my awareness of "fractured narratives" comes more from music than from literature. I am an obsessive record collector, and I know my writing has been influenced by my quirky tastes in pop music. In the fifties, Bill Buchanan and Dickie Goodman popularized the "break-in" novelty record. They would speak the part of reporters asking questions and edit lines of popular songs as the "answers." These interviews playfully fractured listeners' expectations by pulling sources from unexpected places. Buchanan and Goodman made a bunch of flying saucer records, but I remember they were still doing songs in the seventies, with songs about Jaws and Watergate. I even created one of my own break-in songs in a high school media class, where I "spoke" to

Ronald Reagan about the Iran situation, and he "answered" with lines from songs taped from my record collection. My teacher liked the last part of the song best, where I asked Reagan, "What are you going to do tonight after this interview?" and Reagan kept repeating lines from Cheap Trick's "Gonna Raise Hell."

Another kind of fractured recording technique revolves overlaying a familiar narrative with a new or contrasting narrative. In the sixties, producer Phil Spector recorded a Christmas album with all his musical acts and ended side two with a version of "Silent Night." The song featured strings and a choral background while Spector overdubbed his spoken, sincere, almost maudlin, holiday wishes to his listeners. Paul Simon and Art Garfunkel produced a haunting "Silent Night," fractured narrative by overlaying their harmonic lyrics with a monotone news anchor reporting about Vietnam. The simultaneous narratives on these two records create an effect on the listener that goes beyond the traditional versions of "Silent Night."

I also think of movie musicals, where the action is interrupted and enhanced when the performers launch into songs or dance numbers. *A Chorus Line* is a perfect example, where the characters' background and internal mind sets are revealed through their musical numbers: This is information you wouldn't get (or get in the same way) through a more conventional telling. In *Grease*, Olivia Newton-John and John Travolta sing their duet in separate settings, and then in a split-screen shot when their vocals overlap. Elvis Presley movies reveal a similar interweaving of so-called plot with occasions for Elvis to sing so-called plot-related songs. In Presley's movies you change the way you "read" the film, anticipating the next occasion for Elvis to sing rather than wondering what's going to happen next.

Some of my favorite soundtrack albums (which tell their own version of a movie's storyline) play around with fractured narratives. For example, you hear the "Main Theme" from *Star Wars* as the first track, but then you hear the melody as a refrain in several other tracks on the album, almost as a mantra. On the *Chitty Chitty Bang Bang* soundtrack, there are four versions of the title song spaced across the album, sung by different characters from the movie, a technique that depicts how all the characters end up uniting in their fascination for the flying car. And in Harry Nilsson's *The Point!*, Nilsson alternates spoken storytelling with narrative songs, which segue beautifully into each other. (On Nilsson's other soundtrack, *Son of Dracula*, he interweaves actual dialogue from the movie with several of his own musical compositions, a creation that gives such songs as "Daybreak" and "Without You" added layers of meaning.)

What has my interest in these musical "texts" and how they were composed taught me about myself as a writer? Once I began to value how those compositions were created, and began to appreciate a fractured storyline as a feasible, meaningful form, I began to notice that my writing, which I was having difficulty fitting into the "acceptable" structure of written storytelling, might fit a bit more comfortably in an alternate style of fractured narratives. Once, when I was writing in a fiction workshop, I got angry when one of my stories was received so poorly, mainly because—classmates said—it was "good writing," but it "wasn't a story." Even the professor said the story was boring, because it didn't fit into the "inverted check mark" structure, that is, a story begins, it then builds in tension, reaches a climax, then has a short resolution. Using the negative energy from that discussion, I decided to write a story so unstructured that the class couldn't help but hate it. I composed six somewhat autobiographical but still extremely fictional vignettes, or episodes, from different times in a character's life. Not only were the stories out of chronological order, they took chances with unusual internal structures, for example, repeating a piece of dialogue (sort of like I described the *Star Wars* refrain above) within the story, and having one of the characters break out into song (which wasn't received as well). To my surprise, the class and the professor liked the story. I forgot what the professor said (I think I had learned to ignore him), but responders to the story wrote that even though there wasn't a conventional structure to the vignettes, they added up to a whole that left them as readers having feelings that many of them couldn't quite put into words.

I look at the examples above—and the ones I'll share by my students below—as sites for discussion of what we can learn about ourselves and each other as writers and readers. Charles Moran says that what it means to "read like a writer" is to

> understand the writing, the making of the work, at a level so deep that we vicariously participate in its performance. When we read like writers we understand and participate in the writing. We see the choices the writer has made, and we see how the writer has coped with the consequences of those choices. (60–61)

The following excerpts are some of the ways writers in my composition classes and I have taken risks in our writing. I also see them as opportunities for us to practice reading as writers to see what we can learn.

Fractured narratives might be thought of as a kind of literary "juggling" where the writer somehow introduces two or more distinct subjects, voices, or styles, and keeps them alternating (juggling) throughout the narrative. Lisa juggles three subjects in her freewrite "Confusion" by alternating short sentences of different subject matter to convey her boredom with the col-lege routine, her bowling team's exploits, and her continuing disillusionment with a person's betrayal. What do these things have to do with each other? Maybe not much at first, until Lisa juggles them all together in one narrative, and makes us, as readers, come to some sense of how to react. Suddenly, I begin to see how a person may be preoccupied by (here) three concerns, each of varying importance to her. Lisa seems to convey some of the complexity of our minds without using a lot of words to explain herself. She used short sentences in emulation of a story we had just read, Lisa Blaushield's "Witness," which alternated points of views of several witnesses (or people who ignored) a crime.

> It's not fair.
> It's all my fault.
> I need to raise my average.
> Just another day at college.
> If only I could have made that one spare. Then I would be doing good.
> Why did he have to leave? Was it something I did or didn't do?
> Why are we still here? I was looking forward to college until I got here.
> I'm still hurt from it. Is it supposed to hurt for eight years? Maybe it was how he left.
> We have a tournament in a couple of weeks. I hope I can go.
> Did I do something to deserve this hurting?
> We're not ready yet. We need lots of practice.
> I loved my dad. I thought he loved me—I was wrong.
> College is so boring.
> Shouldn't he care about his own daughter more than his new wife's kids?
> My thumb hurts from bowling. Am I doing something wrong?
> I thought college would be fun, different from high school. College is just high school with freedom.
> It doesn't make sense. I didn't know anything was wrong. He just left.
> I can't get rhythm down throwing my new ball. It's supposed to help me raise my average.
> College is OK though. I do have some fun.
> I bowled good at the exhibition we went to, but I can't seem to do it now. Why is that?
> I almost didn't survive. He broke my heart into a million pieces, uncountable.
> Kinda like the stars in the sky. My heart is still broken today.
> I'll never be the same. No one ever is.

I like how Lisa keeps coming back to the bowling as a concern; it makes me think of how we sometimes immerse ourselves in certain activities to take our minds off other, difficult, thoughts. But I also like how she keeps those other, deeper, concerns right there on the page to show how sometimes they just don't go away.

Kelly juggles two texts in an open topic stream of conscious writing, where she weaves lines from the Don Henley song "The End of Innocence" with a description of her mother's reaction to divorce. To me this captures the way lines of a song evoke thoughts in a listener, but it also adds a layer of immediate meaning to that song by punctuating each line with Kelly's own observations. Her writing adds a layer to each of the texts by juggling them together, making each line (for me) "resonate" with meaning.

In conference, Kelly told me she ran out of lines to alternate with the remaining lyrics, so she left the final two by themselves.

Here's my example of juggling two different texts that were already written by somebody else, or "found texts." I found one on the back of an old Paul Petersen album from my record collection, and the other in a *Hollywood Collectables* interview Petersen gave thirty years later. I find it funny how those old albums' liner notes present glowing portraits of "talented new singers" (who often have little actual ability!). I was surprised when I read Petersen's revelations about the limitations he felt from the very profession that had "made" him a star, and I decided to juggle lines from the two texts together.

Paul Petersen is one of today's most versatile and talented recording artists.

Having spent my entire childhood in the fantasy of Hollywood and television, I was totally unprepared to cope with failure in the real world.

With each new album or single release he reaches new heights.

I had no other skills and all my energy had been focused into only one endeavor.

By 1969, I was a total basketcase.

In a matter of weeks the record had become one of the nation's top-selling singles.

I worked 16 weeks in 1966, 4 weeks in 1968 and by 1969, I had no work at all.

What I hoped to accomplish and felt I couldn't accomplish by saying it directly, was how people don't always achieve the goals they'd like to, and sometimes external forces we can't control cause these limitations. See, I don't like how I'm explaining it now; I think the juggled text says better what I was thinking—and that it may say more than that because it offers readers the chance to work at the meanings they get from the narrative.

Another kind of juggling uses certain sentences or sections as a type of "interruption" to fracture the flow of the writing. Sort of like the little beep on those Read 'N' Hear storybook records that tell you to turn the page.

Crissy wrote this fractured narrative called "god revised" using a fragmented style to convey her mixed feelings about the churches she attended and especially about the one she grew up in at Rockaway, New York. Crissy supplies five paragraphs packed with details of people, events, and visions from inside the church, then punctuates each section with a short paragraph that comes straight from the prayers she said. This is another piece I enjoy discussing because we always argue about whether we read the lines as cynical or sincere or a little of both. Here is one segment of Crissy's description followed by its short "punctuating" prayer line (the whole essay can be found in the Appendix).

Church—gothic, beautiful, sad. Stain-glass windows depicting the Stations of the Cross, while the cool sea breeze gently blows through the crack. St. Cammilus, Rockaway. Dark, wood, very hard benches but somehow not so cold. People wear their bathing suits, shorts, and flip-flops to mass, only lasts a half hour. Can't wait to get out and go to the beach. I think Father Burke has the same idea. Funny old man, tells jokes, loves the Mets, sometimes wears a baseball cap. Hard to believe he screamed at my mother during confession when she was twelve, probably drunk, I've seen him at Hickey's.

Peace be with you. And also with you.

Perhaps the most dramatic type of fractured narrative involves juggling different genres in the same piece. Kate juggles genres in "A Broken Hourglass," an essay in which she describes moving out of her father's house and life. She introduces her topic with a letter, then juggles stage dialogue and narrative segments. This was Kate's most innovative piece and came late in the semester, after having taken many risks in other writings, such as experimenting with the letter and dialogue formats. I have "abridged" the entire essay here by including the first line(s) of each section. Even though I leave out a lot of important detail I think you get a sense of the narrative and also see how Kate juggled genres. So I don't interrupt the flow of the sample selections, the genres reflected are 1) letter, 2) narration, 3) dialogue, 4) song quote, 5) narration, 6) dialogue w/narration, and 7) reflective narration.

Dad, I feel like I can't ever do anything right . . .. I feel like everything I do is wrong, and everything Chris does is perfect.

One of my friends, Aimee, let me stay at her house for a few days until I decided what I was going to do. I had no car, clothes, or home. I was completely lost.

Kate: Hey Dad.
Dad: Where are you?
Kate: Don't worry, I'm okay.
Dad: I've been calling all over the town looking for you. For the last time where are you?
Kate: Dad, it's none of your business to know where I am. I don't live there anymore.

"Sometimes we let one another down. Time goes on, people touch and they are gone." (*St. Elmo's Fire*)

Boxes laying everywhere, clothes scattered on the floor, broken picture frames of my dad and I were placed across the room as I packed. I decided to leave and live with my mom. The emptier the room got, the fuller the U-Haul got, and the more my heart broke. I couldn't believe my father gave me a time limit (one day) to decide what I wanted. I felt like an hourglass being turned over. I closed the door of my empty room and walked out.

Three months later, at Kate's sister's wedding, Kate speaks with her dad:

Dad: How are you doing living at mom's?
Kate: Pretty good I guess. But I miss living in Pensacola.
. . . We gave each other a hug and that was pretty much it. The next day
I moved back home with my dad.

*I still have questions about coming back though. Why didn't he call to
talk to me the three months I was gone? Why did he want me back? Was it
because he really cared about me or because it would look good in all the
court cases him and my mom go through? Sometimes I feel like I'm not really
wanted there. I mean my own father hasn't even called me since I've been
away at college. It kind of makes me think if he's looking at the hourglass
waiting for me to come back.*

I don't know if Kate's "sampled" essay has impact on you, but it still reminds
me how this unusually constructed piece made me look at divorce—through
the lens of this particular divorce—in a new way, and how it helped Kate illustrate her own jumbled thoughts in a way she might not have been able without
taking such risks.

In *The Point!* Harry Nilsson tells the story of Oblio, a boy who lived in a
town where everything and everyone had a pointed head, except Oblio.
"Everyone's got 'em," Nilsson sings; that is, a "point." Oblio searches to
discover how to get a point, how to be like everyone else, how to fit in. But in
his quest to find out what's wrong with him, he discovers that it is his difference that gives him his point. On yet another soundtrack in my collection
(*Pufnstuf*), Cass Elliot sings a song called "Different." After worrying that her
abilities set her apart from others, she realizes, "I'd rather be different than be
the same."

In the vein of these artists' songs, I encourage you to tackle some of the
fractured narrative exercises below, with an eye towards defining different ways
of composing them and of possibly creating new techniques of your own.

Exercises

A. Think of an activity you enjoy or dislike immensely. Swimming, writing a paper, walking with headphones on, collecting baseball cards, anything. Do a quick freewrite or list, naming as many specifics about the
activity as possible. Now think of something that might be distracting you
or occupying your mind. Do another freewrite or list. Now take one line
from each and alternate them.

B. Try a "Silent-Night," fractured narrative. Write down as many of the
lyrics as you can, and interrupt the lyrics with a list of your fears or con-

cerns, which contradict the intended mood of the song or with fond memories of your own Christmas pasts, which complement the mood. Try the
technique with other familiar, meaning-laden songs or lyrics such as the
national anthem, the pledge of allegiance, a childhood lullaby, the rules
from a conventional writing textbook.

C. Think of a song that evokes strong feelings or memories for you. Jot
down as many memories as you can while you listen to the song. Play the
song two or three times if that helps. Then copy down lines of the song.
Between each line or verse, insert your actual memories.

D. Think of some speech, slogan, or ad you've heard often and record it
on the page as accurately as you can recall. Or jot down several while
watching TV. Now freewrite sections of prose that contradict or complement those words, using the ads as punctuating lines.

E. Recall an experience that still holds confusion or deep meaning for you.
Break the experience down into genres. For example, begin the narrative
with a letter to one of the people involved, but switch genres for different
scenes. Or revise an essay you have already written by turning it into a
multigenre piece.

Appendix

god revised
by Crissy

Sitting here in church, Ash Wednesday. Christians wear the mark of Christ
upon their foreheads. "Excuse me, you have some dirt on your head." Ashes
to ashes, dust to dust . . . "Ring around the rosy, pocket full of posies, we all
fall down." I see little children, pretty dresses, parents quickly threatening
them to be good. So many old people, too. Maybe praying, asking God for a
couple more years or maybe repenting for all the sins of their bygone days.
Too much regret.

Lord, I am not worthy to receive you but only say the word and I shall be
healed.

Ornate, flashy, gold tabernacle, gold cup, to hold the body and blood of Jesus.
Hard wood pews. Why are they called pews? So cold and hard. Holy water,
cold also. Have you ever looked in the water? I did once, murky, dirty. Ever
since, I only pretend to dip my finger in. Cross thyself; in the name of the
Father, the Son, and the Holy Spirit. Amen.

The Body of Christ. Amen.

I love the crucifix at my church back home, St. Bernadette. Huge, larger than
life, hanging on the wall above the altar. Jesus looks so real, so beautiful.
Almost as though I can see and feel and taste His pain. I can see it on His face,
in His eyes. Such beautiful, sad, tragic eyes. Once I thought I saw tears fall

from His eyes; realized they were mine as I bowed my head and a crystal tear fell to the cold marble floor below.

The blood of Christ. Amen.

Church—gothic, beautiful, sad. Stain-glass windows depicting the Stations of the Cross, while the cool sea breeze gently blows through the crack. St. Cammilus, Rockaway. Dark, wood, very hard benches but somehow not so cold. People wear their bathing suits, shorts, and flip-flops to mass, only lasts a half hour. Can't wait to get out and go to the beach. I think Father Burke has the same idea. Funny old man, tells jokes, loves the Mets, sometimes wears a baseball cap. Hard to believe he screamed at my mother during confession when she was twelve, probably drunk, I've seen him at Hickey's.

Peace be with you. And also with you.

A religion based on one man's life, Jesus Christ, the Son of God, the Light of the World, Our Savior. So much pain, so much sorrow, so much suffering. All for us, all for heaven. We follow Him, we love Him, we are told He loves us. We must follow Him, be His servants. We shall be rewarded in Heaven. The Kingdom of God is ours. Why then so much pain, so much sorrow, so much suffering to those who follow?

Go in peace to love and serve the Lord. Thanks be to God.

Works Cited

Kostal, Irwin, cond. *Chitty Chitty Bang Bang*. LP. United Artists, 1968.

Mohr, Jim. 1994. "A Minor Consideration." *Hollywood Collectibles*. 22–25.

Moran, Charles. 1990. "Reading Like a Writer." *Vital Signs*. Ed. James L. Collins. Portsmouth, NH: Boynton/Cook 60–69.

Nilsson, Harry. 1970. *The Point!* LP. RCA.

Nilsson, Harry. 1973. *Son of Dracula*. LP. Rapple.

Williams, John, comp. 1977. *Star Wars*. LP. Twentieth-Century.

4

Thirteen Ways of Looking
at an Egg
An Assignment in Generation
and Revision

Alys Culhane

I am gathering up my supplies and preparing to teach English 203, "Introduction to Creative Writing," when my office-mate Donna walks into the room. Before me on my desk are pens, overhead transparencies, assignment sheets, freewrites, my journal—and two cartons of eggs.

Noticing the eggs, Donna asks, "Alys, what are you doing with those eggs? Are you going to have an egg toss?"

"No, my students and I are going to write about them."

A look of consternation crosses Donna's smooth forehead. "Why?" she asks.

"It's an experiment, an exercise in observation. I'm thinking that it is when writers abandon their set ideas about form that they come up with some of their best writing," I reply.

Carefully putting the eggs in my backpack, I explain that I'd gotten the idea for the assignment from Robert Persig, the author of *Zen and the Art of Motorcycle Maintenance*. He finds that asking writers to write about small objects such as bricks, quarters, and the backs of their thumbs forces them to come up with something original to say, since they have nothing to imitate.

Donna looks dubious as I head out the door, and this worries me even more. Although I sound confident, I am apprehensive about this assignment.

My fears are related to the fact that I'm not sure what, if anything, my students and I will learn about writing. To reassure myself, I take deep breaths and remind myself that the best writing comes about when writers take risks—and that, for sure, is what we are going to be doing this particular semester.

Take This Fish and Look at It

Most of the day's class is conventional. We spend the majority of our time freewriting and discussing Samuel Scudder's "Take This Fish and Look at It." In "Take This Fish," Scudder gives an account of his experiences as a student observer. He goes to study with Louis Agassiz, a well known and respected professor of natural history. Scudder hopes that Agassiz will teach him more about entomology. However, after Agassiz asks Scudder a few questions, he gives him a fish, a haemulon, and tells him to observe it. As Scudder learns in this three-day exercise, "seeing" involves "looking."

In our discussion of the Scudder essay, many valid points are made. Some feel that Agassiz is asking for trouble by having an entomology student observe a fish. Others think that Scudder is equally insane for going along with Agassiz's plan.

"What would you do if you found yourself in Agassiz's class and were asked to observe a fish?" I ask.

"I'm a business major. I'd drop the course," says Ken.

"What if it was, like this course, a general education requirement?" Michael asks.

"I guess I'd have to learn to like fish," says Ken.

Others saw the merit of Agassiz's observation exercise.

Roger says that the story showed the importance of detail. And Amy, making the connections between observation and art, suggests that "many artists have probably been asked by their teachers to do exercises that at first they did not understand."

Barb had a take that makes for a good segue into the egg exercise. She notes that in a previous creative writing class, she and her classmates were asked to observe pine cones for two weeks, and to enter their observations into their journals. Making a comparison to Scudder's situation, she reads a portion of her freewrite out loud:

> I could identify with Scudder's reluctance to perform the task and or at least his lack of understanding in the beginning. But like me, not only did he discover and learn more about the fish (pine cone), but he also learned more about himself. He discovered how writing motivates and enhances the discovery process and is actually a powerful way of thinking. The professor substantiates that when he says that "a pencil is one of the best of eyes . . ." I discovered observing the pine cone that the more I discovered the more I wanted to discover. It became exciting and challenging to learn more than I had previously known.

A conversation about Barb's freewrite follows her reading. The writers are incredulous that Barb's former creative writing teacher had the nerve to ask her students to carry around and write about a pine cone. And they are surprised to see that she saw it as being a positive experience.

"Better you than me," says Sammy, shaking his head.

A lull in the conversation. I reach into my knapsack and pull out the eggs. Seeing the carton, the class collectively emits a loud groan.

"We aren't going to be writing about eggs, are we?" asks Sammy.

"I'd rather write about pine cones," says Ben.

Ignoring these and other remarks, I stride around the inside of the circle, and with great ceremony, have each writer choose an egg. Some deliberate, while others quickly make their choices. I then give a brief overview of the entire assignment, and a specific exercise for the next class.

"For the next six weeks we'll observe these eggs. And in the following six weeks we'll use your data in our revisions. So keep your egg with you at all times, and of course, bring it to class," I say.

I also caution writers that they were not intentionally to fold, spindle, or in any way mutilate their eggs. I add, "If your egg breaks, put its remains in an airtight container. Or get another egg. The most important thing is that you continue your observations."

"I can't carry this egg around with me all the time. I work in a factory," says Ken.

"Hire an egg sitter," suggests Michael.

"And write about it," I add.

"If I'm seen carrying this egg around, I'll be labeled the dorm idiot," wails Trish.

"They'll be envious once they learn that you are doing a class assignment," I reply.

The class ending, I explain that the assignment for the following Thursday is to come up with 50 direct observations about the egg. The students again look aghast.

"Its brown, round, and came from a chicken," says Sammy, tossing his egg up and down in his hand.

"Hey, yours looks just like mine," says Ken.

Looking at my own brown, round chicken egg, I don't see much more than Sammy or Ken do. Like them, I realize that I too am going to have to be pushing my powers of observation.

In- and Out-of-Class Exercises

For the next four sessions, we come to class with 50 observations or 200 total for each observer. And we began each meeting by telling one another three unusual things about our eggs. The only rule is, no one can repeat an already given observation. Predictably, the first few responses elicit the usual observations: chicken eggs are brown, odorless, oval, flavorless, filled with yoke, and have hard shells. Mixed with these responses, however, are more unusual ones. One writer notes that the shell of her egg is thicker at one end than the other. Another tells us that her egg has craters at one end. And I mention that my egg is brown in some places and pinkish-grey in others.

In the subsequent classes, our responses become more detailed. Finding that we have to push ourselves to come up with (no pun) fresh ideas, we begin experimenting. Eggs are rolled, measured, weighed, spun, poked, and dropped onto soft surfaces. Some apply various substances, such as ink, bleach, magic marker, vinegar, Vaseline, and crayon to their eggs. And they subsequently attempt to remove these markings with various types of stain removers. (We learn that Pinesol removes crayon and pencil marks but does not remove indelible marker.) We also discover that:

- When water is poured on an egg, it runs off.
- It (the egg) falls on its side, if you try to balance it on its points.
- When you spin an egg and squint, it looks like a blurry mass, like the lava inside a lava-dome lamp.
- It fits in the top of a trumpet.
- Scotch tape is easy to remove if applied to the surface of an egg.

We also made some rather imaginative associations:

- The bumps feel like Braille markings for the blind.
- My egg smells like rubber.
- It has dimples like a golf ball.
- It might sound dumb, but my egg smells like Easter.
- When I put the egg in a bowl of hot water, bubbles form on the surface of the egg. The bubbles look like fish eyes.

Our findings are not limited to direct observations. We write puns and make comparisons, such as, my egg is like a _____ because _____.
Some of the more novel of these comparisons include:

- My egg is like a Republican because it is brain dead.
- My egg is like someone with a hot temper because it is hard-boiled.
- An egg is like a water balloon dipped in dilute cement.
- An egg is like a safe because it holds something inside until cracked.
- An egg is like a record because it is easily broken.

The observations also evoke memories:

- When I was a kid, I used to draw pictures of people and their heads would look similar to the shape of this egg. The top of the head was bigger than the bottom.
- When I look at this egg it makes me think of my 86-year-old grandmother. She will not make eggs without picking out the white membranes attached to the yoke.

Intrigued by these and other findings, we ask one another questions and make like-observations. For example, we as a class collectively discover that some of us can fit our eggs into our mouths and some of us can not. And in an attempt to determine if eggs all spin at the same rate of speed, we have Kurt and Kyle (identical twins) get down on the floor, spin their eggs, then exchange them. (Through this controlled experiment, we determine that no two eggs spin at the same rate of speed.)

In addition to doing out-of-class observations, we complete numerous in-class egg exercises including looping, cubing, and clustering. Another exercise includes writing for twenty minutes about a "bad egg." We also describe our eggs to an alien, write lists of how we'll dispose of our eggs, and write radio advertisements in which we try to sell our eggs. After six weeks of observing eggs, those who still have intact eggs take them to the edge of the local woods and hit them with golf clubs.

Not only do we as writers generate a great deal of useful material, but the aforementioned assignments also bring about some very interesting digressions. And, believing that verbal narratives inspire good writing, I encourage talk. Some of the observations lead to discussions about what it's like to be different, the responsibilities of being a parent, the pros and cons of abortion, the ethics of recycling, and the necessity of violence. (This topic inspired by Amy, who wisely noted that most of the suggestions for getting rid of eggs are violent.) And the question, do chicken have teeth? starts what I eventually call our "collective oral history"—an ongoing discussion of our dental histories.

Richard Hugo's Triggering Town: From Generation to Revision

The first half of the six-week assignment being over, we each have approximately seventy-five pages of observations. Understandably, we are all nervous going into the second half of this assignment. It is one thing to generate ideas, but it is quite another to do something with them. How, we wonder, might we make the great leap from unfinished to finished work? Fortunately, I had chosen Richard Hugo's *Triggering Town* as a course text. At the beginning of the semester I'd reasoned that since Hugo's text had been beneficial in terms of my own understanding of revision, others would also find it useful. Also, I liked the way that Hugo used his writing to make his point—that writers' ideas often change as they compose their texts. My intuitive and somewhat arbitrary choice proves to be the right one. After we read the book, I begin the second six-week segment of this assignment by asking, what is Hugo saying about revision and how might it be applicable to us as writers?

In the subsequent class discussions, the class correctly defines a "trigger" as an idea that is a catalyst for another idea. Furthermore, we note how in his work, Hugo uses the metaphors of place and memory to move from one idea to the next. We also talk at length about our own revising processes. I admit that I am an overly compulsive reviser and will routinely do twenty or thirty drafts of an essay. By way of example, I pass around the ten drafts of my bad egg prose-poem. "I'm trying to be less critical of my work, and to revise less," I say. My confession opens the door to further conversation since a few class members say that they have never been encouraged to revise extensively and, further, are reluctant to do so. As Jill admits, "I'd rather write a paper the night before and get a C than possibly revise it and get the same grade. Because if I revise it and get a C, that would be proof that I'm not all that good a writer." Acknowledging Jill's comment, I add that in general, revision is risky because much of the time, writers don't know what they are going to end up with.

Using Hugo's text as a "trigger" to talk about revision also enables me to put what we will do for the next six weeks into context. On Tuesdays we refer to course readings in an attempt to define the characteristics of poetry, prose poetry, fiction, and nonfiction. And on Thursdays, we workshop. I stress that in their revisions writers needn't stick to the topic of the egg, but use the egg, as Hugo did, as a trigger, to generate other ideas. I also carefully explain that, in part, our job as workshoppers/audience members is to help one another make these metaphorical and associative leaps. This input, I say, will make it easier for us to produce approximately twenty pages of finished writing (in any genre) by the semester's end and we'll select our best work for inclusion in a class book.

During the next six weeks, we assist one another in finding our writing triggers. We read one another's journal entries, conference, and note down what interests us as readers. One class exercise involves putting a list of "triggers" and "topics" on the board:

Trigger	Topics
poaching	illegal hunting
dropping	dropping out of school
fear of heights	airplanes
bad eggs	stink bombs in the dorms
Uncle Ted	grade school enemies
raw eggs	Rambo, macho guys
fits in a shotglass	Drunks, underage drinking

During the second half of the semester there are no complaints about not having anything to write about, nor are there any problems with determining what genre a given work might fit into. In fact, because there are no limitations put on length, form, or genre the majority of us feel freer to experiment.

In part, I attribute our high degree of revisionary flexibility to the fact that our definitional discussions complement what takes place in the workshop sessions. Our reading-related conversations focus as much on the commonalties inherent to these genres as they do on the differences—we agree, good poetry, fiction, and nonfiction contain description, detail, voice, is metaphorical, and is subject to multiple interpretations. Moreover, we are quick to point out to one another when our own work exhibits these characteristics.

The Final Products

As writers, we become more confident about generating our own ideas, and as revisers, we began taking more risks. Even though the assignment is difficult (and some think too lengthy), it enables us to produce some of our best work. This becomes evident when we flip through the pages of our completed class books. The representative samples that follow illustrate how we adhered to and, at the same time, pushed the boundaries of poetic convention.

The trigger for Matt Kasper's prose poem is hatred. In his original writing, he began by writing about how he hated eggs and went on to write about how he hated red lights.

The Power of the Lights

I see the red light. I feel the strength this red light has. My mind, my body, and my car are trained to be stopped by it. We are all trained. Red is anger. We see red. Red alarms us. We turn red. Blood is red. Red is fear. Put all that into a bright light. That is power—the light restrains me, it restrains everyone. The opposite "don't walk" sign is not even flashing. My stereo has been stolen yet my foot is tapping uncontrollably. I hate thieves. Right now, I hate everyone. I wish I were here only for an eternity. I could only be so lucky.

An anonymous tinted window pulls up next to me. I hate faceless people. The road funnels from two lanes into one. Pole position is what we both want. I will win!—"Don't walk" is flashing now. The red light holds me still. The opposite light turned yellow. The red light will not budge. I anticipate the downfall of the red and the rising of the green. The opposite light is red now. Mine is still red, but I can feel it get weaker. I can crawl forward just a bit. IT'S FINALLY GREEN! Green freedom, green power, Green Peace, Green Lantern, a Green Bay Packer victory. I love green. It slings me forward like a catapult. I win. A thousand white doves have been released and trumpets are playing. I see another red light but I ride this high right through its barriers. A red light now flashes in my rearview mirror.

Memories of his grandmother's cooking trigger Roger Schimberg's prose-poem.

Patiently Waiting

It takes her forever to walk to the coop. I tell her to hurry. She walks slowly, one foot then another. The chickens are hungry and so am I.

"They're cluckin' away grandma."

"So are you," she tells me.

Her way of taking everything in as she walks frustrates me.

I'm in my youth. I walk fast.

"What are you looking at, grandma?"

She tells me that she is looking at life. I don't understand.
What is there to look at? What hasn't she seen before?
"Lets go grandma, how many eggs for French toast, how many for an omelet? That sounds even better."
She has always walked through life patient, looking. Those old shoes, worn through the heels from years of work on the farm.
They'll step a few more months, then no more walks to the coop.
"Come on grandma, what are you waiting for?"
"I'm just looking at life."
Now I understand.

When my egg broke in my carton, I began writing about the mess in the carton—the end result, this prose poem:

The Dumpster Diver

Shaking an egg carton, the old man begins dancing. His sunglasses balanced on the edge of his nose, he stretches his arms outward, and wiggles his fingers. The cat, balancing on the dumpster ledge, flicks her tail and dives into a cardboard box. He knows that to grow, to become strong and healthy, you need equal parts sunlight and water. But how do you collect sunlight if you don't have a spoon? As the God Lord has told him, "you dance until the sun goes down." He knows this as he knows that the wind will whistle at the women who ignore his curious glances.

And, although she plays with the form of this poem, and experiments with line breaks and stanzas, Barb Hyder's group members liked this, the original draft of her concrete poem:

13 Ways of Looking at an Egg

albino rock
beneath a chicken
armor for an infant fowl
with my hashbrowns, toast, and coffee
cradled in an apron fresh from the hen house
teenage pockets like squirrel cheeks at homecoming
a forgotten Christmas wreath the birds call home
a vessel carrying Mork to Mindy from Ork
brightly colored in a basket at Easter
delicate and fragile as crystal
cracking under pressure
a brain on drugs
in a dozen.

Works Cited

Hugo, Richard. 1979. *The Triggering Town: Lectures and Essays on Poetry and Writing*. New York, NY: Norton.

Persig, Robert. 1980. *Zen and the Art of Motorcycle Maintenance.* New York, NY: Bantam.

Scudder, Samuel. 1983. "Take This Fish and Look at It." *Readings for Writers.* 4th ed. Ed. Jo Ray McCuen and Anthony C. Winkler. New York, NY: Harcourt, 82–86.

5

The Case for Double-Voiced Discourse

Lad Tobin

Most composition textbooks make writing sound a little like trying to defuse a bomb: be careful, new writers are told, if you make a mistake, if you don't follow the proper protocol, it all could blow up in your face. And so these books proceed according to that old medical motto: First Do No Harm. In a voice that manages to sound alternately grouchy, prissy, moralistic, and deferential (but still somehow never quite human), the authors of these books want to make sure that student writers understand that an essay is not a place to relax or goof around or mess up. The message is sobering: readers are grim, busy, and potentially vindictive people who do not gladly suffer fools.

Of course, that's where the textbooks, handbooks, style sheets, and writing teachers enter the scene: don't try this at home, they warn new writers—unless you are willing to follow basic rules and regulations, such as "Stick to one central point throughout the essay" or "Omit unnecessary words." Now these rules seem reasonable—and harmless—enough. After all, who can argue with clarity and efficiency? And if you are writing a lab report, book review, or essay exam, these rules might serve you well. (Of course, if you are writing for a teacher who swears by these rules, they certainly will serve you well.)

One problem, though, is that these rules make it seem as if writers are always limited to either/or choices: clarity or fuzziness, correctness or incorrectness, efficiency or wasted time, good writing or bad. In fact, alternative styles—which can be indirect, which can violate certain rules of grammar and usage, which can allow for digression, play, and self-expression—may actually be more effective in certain writing situations.

I hated writing when I was a student. At least I hated school writing. The only essays I remember writing for teachers were stale, canned five-paragraph exercises—with one exception: it was a piece I wrote in second grade that I still remember all these years later. The essay began with me telling the reader that I was an eight-year-old boy (which I was) who had snuck a transistor radio into my classroom to listen to the World Series (which I wished I had done but hadn't). The "essay" was really just an excuse for me to do in school what I would always do at home—fantasize about baseball players and statistics. Ninety percent of the essay was a word-by-word description of the supposed radio announcer's play-by-play of the game. As in, "Stan Musial is up to bat, runner on second, two outs. Billy Pierce is on the mound, He wheels, he deals. Musial swings and hits a high lazy fly ball to left field." And so on, for pages and pages.

I had some reason to think that Mrs. Partlow, my second grade teacher, might not entirely mind this subject matter: I had heard through the grapevine that her younger brother was a major league ball player, Danny Litwiler, the center fielder for the St Louis Cardinals. Still, I must have sensed that even a sympathetic reader might lose patience or consciousness reading through nine innings of straight play-by-play narrative.

So I made a writerly decision: I broke up the radio announcer's play-by-play of the game with a dramatic story about how worried I was that Mrs. Partlow would spot the radio and take it away. As the game went on and became more and more dramatic, so did the close encounters I was having trying to keep the radio concealed. The last scene: The ninth inning. The Cardinals load the bases. Two outs. Just then Mrs. Partlow spots the radio and demands that I give it to her. But when I tell her that the batter is—who else?—Danny Litwiler!!—she relents and decides to let the whole class listen. Now here the family legend is a little fuzzy. My own memory is that I was such a diehard Sox fan that I wrote that Litwiler's long drive was caught at the wall by Minnie Minoso. My brother's memory is that I was such a little kiss-up that the ball ticked off Minoso's glove for a grand slam home run.

Once people start making up rules, they don't know when to stop—and that can be another problem. So, in some textbooks, the rule about writing clearly grows into "Don't write in a way that calls attention to yourself or your writing," and the one about providing evidence turns into "Don't be too personal." In fact, this argument that writers should develop a style that is somehow unobtrusive, transparent, impersonal, and consistent is one of the most pervasive and dreary ideas running through the advice writers give writing students. Listen:

> Write in a way that draws the reader's attention to the sense and substance of the writing, rather than to the mood and temper of the author . . . . To achieve style, begin by affecting none—that is, place yourself in the background. (Strunk and White, 70).

> All successful writing shares one feature—clarity. Clear writing begins with clear thinking; clear thinking begins with an understanding of what all the terms mean. Therefore, clear writing begins with definitions that both reader and writer understand. (Lannon, 329)

> Don't show off; avoid drawing unnecessary attention to yourself. Stick to the business of telling readers what you know. When we blatantly insert ourselves into our story, we are like thoughtless people who invite friends to a movie and then spend so much time talking that they can't enjoy the show. (Marius, 195)

Again, this advice sounds reasonable in a way. Be polite and conscientious, these authors tell student writers, or your readers will be offended, bored, and, according to William Zinsser, anxious.

> Unity is the anchor of all good writing. So, first of all, get your unities straight. Unity not only keeps the reader from straggling off in all directions; it satisfies the reader's subconscious need for order and gives reassurance that all is well at the helm. (49–50)

Now while it is certainly true that readers may lose interest in an essay that rambles on endlessly and pointlessly about any and every odd thing the writer thought or did, it is also true that we have all read essays that were too polite, too impersonal, too flat to hold our interest, just as we have all seen movies we never would have enjoyed if we hadn't been able to make fun of them with our friends.

The conventional elements of style used to make a lot of sense to me. Take the notions of unity and consistency. When I was in college in the early seventies, my English teachers believed that all the great canonical texts that they taught (*Hamlet* or *A Rose for Emily* or *Ode on a Grecian Urn*) were, by definition, unified and consistent. Devoted "new critics," they believed that every scene and character, every metric beat or symbolic reference, was there for a reason, contributed to a single unified effect, and—with great effort and proper training—could be identified and explained.

My teachers were equally confident about their reading of our essays. Of course, our essays could never achieve the exquisite order, balance, and control of literary texts, but they could still aim to become unified, coherent wholes with clear thesis statements, definite transitions, logical supporting points. These teachers, living in a pre- postmodern world, believed that written texts, like the world itself, followed a certain logical order.

And as an eager to please undergraduate English major, I bought it all: with my Strunk and White in one hand and the essays of Samuel Johnson in the other, I decided that there was a clear right and wrong way to write and I learned quickly that dissension, dissonance, loose ends were in the wrong column. It worked—in a way: I got good grades on my essays. But somewhere along the line, my firm opinions and beliefs about truth, beauty, and good writing started to fall apart because, first, I started reading wonderful novels and essays that didn't adhere to the conventions and, second, I realized that the rigidity of the rules never allowed me to write in a way that reflected the way my mind actually worked.

Underneath the elements of conventional style is a controlling and questionable belief: that all good essays are unified and consistent. There is the notion that an essay should be like a seamless web, that it should move from point to point in a fluid, linear motion, that a writer should never use "I," that every thesis statement needs three supporting points, every supporting point needs three supporting details. That idea represents a particular sort of style. At its best that style produces readable, logical essays; at its worst, it produces writing with all the panache of a tax form. ("A Place for Everything and Everything in its Place" could be another textbook motto.)

When I ask, my students usually tell me that a good essay is one that "flows." I think they mean that a good essay shouldn't stop and start, dip and dart, jump up or fall off. It shouldn't call attention to its parts to the detriment of its whole. It shouldn't be choppy, blocky, frozen, or dammed up. It should make sense, hang together. It should . . . flow. Fine, I want to answer, but remember: there are flows and there are flows. The kind most of us have been trained to read and respect are mechanical flows that rely on carefully structured arguments, coherent paragraphs, and clear transitions to move the piece along, while the kind I find myself increasingly attracted to are more natural flows that move, as the mind moves, through a series of unconscious associations of words, images, and ideas.

Like the Johnsonian balanced sentence or the heroic rhymed couplet, the elements of conventional style were designed for a different world than the one we live in now. If style is supposed to be an expression of the writer's "natural" (as opposed to artificial) self, then it should be multidimensional, nonlinear and, to use a term of the Russian critic and philosopher Bakhtin, *heteroglossic*. Essays should reflect the way we think and experience the world. And the fact is, we often think and experience the world in a multidimensional, multivoiced way.

When I started teaching, I insisted on thesis statements, explicit transitions, clear supporting paragraphs. I started talking about order and unity and consistency. The fact is, I started doing all the things to my students that my high school teachers did to me. But then something happened; I was reading a batch of essays written in my Advanced Comp class. Each argument, narrative, and description was clearly organized, straightforward, unified, consistent. Each writer's tone was modulated and reasonable. Each transition made sense. In fact, these essays had none of the problems that teachers usually complain about: there were no obvious or nagging problems with grammar or usage; there were no glaring inconsistencies in tone or diction; there were no jarring or contrived transitions. The writing was understated, never showy, never performative. There was nothing to distract the reader, to catch his or her eye. Nothing to call attention to itself. No subheads. No stops and starts. No digressions.

I should have been happy. These were just the sort of essays that Miss Palmer, my high school English teacher, would have been proud to receive. In fact, these were wildly successful examples of almost everything I was taught when I was in high school and college English classes. You could almost see the handbooks, textbooks, and stylesheets peeking out behind these essays and their authors. (Like this: "Although Senate Appropriations Bill 327 might seem at first glance to put an undue burden on American taxpayers, there are political, economic, and ethical reasons to support it.")

But maybe that success was part of the problem. The essays were too neat, too logical, too seamless. I found myself craving surprises, shifts, bounces. I yearned for messiness. And yet I couldn't quite figure out how to advise my students to untidy their pieces. The stories seemed so coherent, so unified, so finished, that I couldn't find a gap to explore or a contradiction to deconstruct.

Of course, it's not easy to tell students to write less coherently, less logically. It seems perverse. After years of being told to embrace consistency, logic, clarity, uniformity, students would have every right to throw up their hands (or their lunches) if a teacher complained, "I want something messier." But the fact is, much of the writing I was reading was just too neat, too logical, too predictable.

You have probably read novels, such as James Joyce's *Ulysses* or William Faulkner's *The Sound and the Fury*, that shift between various narrative perspectives. By using multiple voices, these novelists create tension and drama and demonstrate how much point of view shapes our view of reality. But it is not only fiction writers who make use of multivoiced discourses; increasingly contemporary nonfiction writers—as well as screenwriters, advertisers, and emailers—are turning to double- or multivoiced discourses to represent experience.

Creating two or more voices and perspectives, the multivoiced discourse disrupts the conventional rules about consistency. It does not aim for the seamlessness that most conventional textbooks advocate but instead seeks to make use of the seams. Instead of using explicit transitions (such as, "The new Honda Prelude not only offers the serious driver excellent acceleration and handling, it also comes equipped with top of the line anti-lock brakes."), the multivoiced writer might shift from one voice, consciousness, or perspective through implicit or symbolic connections.

To avoid accidents—or sometimes to create them—good essays often need to break without warning, change lanes without signaling, accelerate without conscience.

Like the metaphysical poets, multivoiced writers often seek to link ideas, events, people, places that do not immediately seem connected or even related. John McPhee, the acclaimed nonfiction writer, explains the power and value of this sort of juxtaposition.

> Structure is the juxtaposition of parts, the way in which two parts of a piece of writing merely by lying side-by-side, can comment on each other without a word spoken. The way in which the thing is assembled, you can get much said, which can be lying there in the structure of the piece rather than being spelled out by a writer. (Sims, 13)

There are a number of different multidimensional structures; nonfiction writers juxtapose external action and internal analysis, description and argument, narrative and fantasy, past and present. This sort of writing has a cinematic feel in which scenes are edited to comment on each other without a voiceover narrator needing to tell us that we have made the shift. These essays are built on juxtaposition rather than direct connection, on the tension between two or more voices, points of view, time frames.

While these pieces are less rigidly controlled than conventional essays, they are not without some sort of guiding structure or organization. Often, the essay is held together not *in spite* of the tension between the two different voices but *because* of that tension.

Some Types of Double-Voiced Narratives

Many conventional essays suffer from their single-mindedness. The writer has done a fine job of narrating an event of describing a person or place, but the piece seems overly flat and listless. By juxtaposing that same narrative with any number of other perspectives, it suddenly becomes richer, more evocative, and compelling. Here, by way of example, are three of the most common double-voiced narratives.

Past and Present

In one of his first books, *The Levels of the Game*, McPhee juxtaposes—and shifts back and forth between—a game-by-game description of a singles tennis match (the 1971 US Open between Arthur Ashe and Clark Graebner), which covers just two hours and biographical profiles of the players, which cover huge amounts of time and space. So while one voice or narrative perspective describes a particular point in which Graebner plays a series of conservative shots as opposed to the higher risk returns that Ashe makes, the other voice breaks in to talk about the risks that Ashe took as an African American teenager playing tennis on public courts in Virginia.

One advantage of such a structure is that the chronological narrative is straightforward and linear and holds the piece tightly together. Since the chronological frame tethers the piece to the ground, the other time frame (McPhee has referred to this technique as "contrapunctual time") can be much freer and looser without risking the confusion of the reader.

External Action and Internal Consciousness

Think of this like the television program, *The Wonder Years*, in which the text moves back and forth between third-person action and first-person reminiscences, opinions, and analysis. Or maybe it is more like another television show, *Mystery Science Theatre*, on the Comedy Channel, in which a man and two aliens sit in the first row of a movie theatre making fun of the movie on the screen. The pleasure is provided by the interplay between the voice and action of the movie and the sarcastic comments of the three commentators. In any case, one voice or tone tends to be relatively straightforward, while the other problematizes the original in some way.

This internal voice usually offers a personal perspective on the narrated events. "The introduction of a personal voice," according to the literary journalist Mark Kramer (Sims, 17), "allows the writer to play one world off against another, to toy with irony." Often this internal voice is set off from the external action by white space or the use of an italic or bold typeface. Take this example of student writing from a student at my university.

> My father was fourteen. He swore he would never be like that. Then he began
> to drink and use drugs. He would neglect and abuse his family. He's never
> gone into detail about his drinking. He hates that part of his life. He sobered
> up sixteen years ago. He didn't want to lose control anymore. He couldn't
> help acting like his father. It's hereditary.
>
>   It is hereditary?

I could never imagine my father hitting me.

When I was in the sixth grade I remember going to visit my brother . . .
(B. D., 39)

In other texts the shift from the journalistic objectivity to personal reflection is subtle and unmarked typographically. For example, in Kramer's study
of a cancer surgeon, Russell Stearne, the dominant voice is third person, historical narrative. But at key moments, Kramer's own voice intervenes.

Stearne dictates his record of her visit at once. It ends with the curious sentence: "Prognosis, of course, guarded." The prognosis, is, of course, death.
And what is guarded is Stearne. (Sims, 150)

Or in nature writer David Quammen's essay "Strawberries Under Ice," he moves
back and forth between a scientific study of ice and highly personal confes-
sions about his own associations.

We think of iciness as a synonym for cold but cold is relative and ice happens
to function well as insulation against heat loss: low thermal conductivity. Also
it *releases* heat to immediate surroundings in the final stage of becoming frozen itself. Ice warms. On a certain night, roughly thirteen years ago, it warmed
me. (212)

Historical Reality and Symbolic Reality

Like poets or novelists, good essayists may invent, develop or identify actions,
characters, and places that represent abstract ideas or feeling states. So you end
up with an essay that shifts back and forth between straightforward exposition
and some sort of sustained symbolic action.

For example, in her essay, "Silent Dancing," Judith Ortiz Cofer moves back
and forth between exposition about her Puerto Rican New York childhood and
italicized images from home movies of her parents and older relatives.

My father's Navy check provided us with financial security and a standard of
living that the factory workers envied. The only thing his money could not
buy us was a place to live away from the barrio—his greatest wish, Mother's
greatest fear.

*In the home movie the men are shown next, sitting around a card table
set up in one corner of the living room, playing dominoes . . . .* (21)

Or take a look at Judy Ruiz's "Oranges and Sweet Sister Boy" in which
she cuts between an autobiographical narrative and a series of dreams or hal-
lucinations.

My children used to ask me to "start" their oranges for them. That meant to
make a hole in the orange so they could peel the rind away, and their small
hands weren't equipped with fingernails that were long enough or strong

enough to do the job. Sometimes they would suck the juice out of the hole my thumbnail had made, leaving the orange flat and sad.

The earrings are as big as dessert plates, filigree gold-plated with thin dangles hanging down that touch her bare shoulders. She stands in front of the Alamo while a bald man takes a picture . . . . (226)

Finally, consider this example from Sarah Davidson's "Real Property" in which she raises a question about what is "real" about the real estate boom in southern California in the 1980s, by suddenly introducing a striking image from a trip she took to an Israeli kibbutz.

Gidon, who is twenty-eight, has two daughters and a newborn son. "Who says children take away your freedom? I have a family, and my work, and tell me, what is a career,"—he held up his baby son—"compared to this?"

HAVE A GOOD TOMORROW,
BUY REAL ESTATE TODAY.
—a billboard in Marina Del Rey

"Six months after I moved into my house in Venice—the house for which everyone thought I had paid too much—realtors began to knock on my door and ask if I wanted to sell." (Sims, 206)

Writing a Double-Voiced Narrative

It is difficult enough to control a single narrative, and you may find it almost impossible to develop a double-voiced narrative in your first draft. It will probably feel easier to try to write a single-voiced narrative in your first draft, then free associate to find possible second voices and perspectives. Play with time, place, point of view, and narrative perspective.

Once you choose one that seems promising, try to write a number of scenes or reflections in that voice without worrying about exactly how they will fit into the essay. Then in a revision, use the "cut and paste" feature on your word processor (or scissors and tape, if you prefer) to splice in pieces from the second consciousness. Though your transitions do not need to be explicit, there ought to be an associative or symbolic connections between the two discourses.

I just got a batch of double-voiced essays from my advanced comp students: one writer moves back and forth between a narrative about the time a driver hit a deer in front of her house and painful memories from her own childhood; another juxtaposes descriptions of vivid nightmares she had been having with national statistics about violence against women; a third cuts back and forth between a description of a weekend hike in the White Mountains of New Hampshire and a carefully detailed research project on the Native Americans who lived in the mountains 100 years ago. The essays are risky, unconventional, and filled with striking and

original unions of unlikely images and ideas. Still, even as I struggle to relax, most of these essays strike me as downright confusing, disjointed, and disorganized. I pick up a red pen and turn my attention to one particularly troubling essay in which the two voices seem completely unconnected to me. I am tempted to write the author a fussy note about the need for thesis statements and clear transitions, about how, as a grim, busy, and vindictive person who does not gladly suffer fools, I don't have time to waste on an essay I can't follow.

But the more I think about why it doesn't work, the more I see suggestive connections lurking between the voices and beneath the lines. I use the red pen to make two notes: one to remind my students that their two voices ought to create a productive, intentional, and coherent tension; the other to remind myself that double-voiced discourses often require double-eared readings.

Works Cited

B.D. 1994. "Flow." *Fresh Ink: Essays From Boston College's First-Year Writing Seminar.* Eds. Lad Tobin and Eileen Donovan-Kranz. Chestnut Hill, MA: Boston College. 39–41.

Cofer, Judith Ortiz. 1991. "Silent Dancing." *The Best American Essays 1991.* Ed. Joyce Carol Oates. New York, NY: Ticknor & Fields. 17–25.

Davidson, Sarah. 1984. "Real Property." *The Literary Journalists.* Ed. Norman Sims. New York, NY: Ballantine. 187–212.

Kramer, Mark. 1984. "Invasive Procedures." *The Literary Journalists.* Ed. Norman Sims. New York, NY: Ballantine. 145–62.

Lannon, John. 1995. *The Writing Process: A Concise Rhetoric.* 5th ed. New York, NY: Harper-Collins.

Marius, Richard. 1995. *A Writer's Companion.* 3rd ed. New York, NY: McGraw-Hill.

McPhee, John. 1989. *Levels of the Game.* New York: Farrar, Straus & Giroux.

Quammen, David. 1989. "Strawberries Under Ice." *The Best American Essay 1989.* Ed. Geoffrey Wolff. New York, NY: Ticknor & Fields. 212–224.

Ruiz, Judy. 1989. "Oranges and Sweet and Sister Boy." *The Best American Essay 1989.* Ed. Geoffrey Wolff. New York, NY: Ticknor & Fields. 225–233.

Sims, Norman. ed. 1984. *The Literary Journalists.* New York, NY: Ballantine.

Strunck, William and E. B. White. 1972. *The Elements of Style.* 2nd ed. New York, NY: Macmillan.

Zinsser, William. 1995. *On Writing Well.* 5th ed. New York, NY: HarperCollins.

6

Why Writers Relish Research
Alternative Writing Projects

Amy Cashulette Flagg

One of the first research papers I can remember writing was in eleventh grade. We were told to pick any topic pertaining to biology and follow the directions of our English teacher. Our biology teacher was to grade the content, and our English teacher was to grade the writing and correctness. I chose to write my paper on the secrets of Acupuncture. This was a traditional approach to writing a research paper—we had to have a thesis statement, an outline with topic sentences, and note cards with all the quotes we had pulled from other sources. I found these checkpoints tedious, but I enjoyed finding out about this topic and included many diagrams and other interesting pictures in my final draft. For each of these I wrote a caption.

I remember finishing the paper the night before it was due and getting my mom to stay up and type it so I could go to bed. I was excited, if not pleased, with my paper and expected positive feedback at least for the information it contained. I didn't care so much about the correctness because even when I took the time to edit carefully my English teacher was always able to ferret out many mistakes.

I wish I had that paper with me now rather than working from memory, but apparently my biology and English teachers found the topic less than interesting. At least, it didn't elicit comments from either. Just marks that showed I fell short on this exercise. They thought the captioned pictures were just filler, even though one showed all the acupuncture points on the human body. I realized this paper was like a lot of work we had to do in school—it was just a practice exercise—it wasn't designed to be interesting. I was never a disciplined student, good grades were not a particularly motivating goal for me, and now with the realization that even what I found interesting was just another assignment, I began to dread the annual research paper even more. It was a long, boring task designed to teach me how to use footnotes and to create flawless bibliography pages. I wondered why the teachers didn't just assign topics that they were interested in. (I suspect now that acupuncture wasn't the sort of topic my high school teachers expected for a formal, academic research paper.)

As an undergraduate English major I thought of research as literary studies. Even though I had a journalism minor I never thought of working on stories as research. Later I realized my work in both these areas was research and each were guided by similar goals and needs. In writing about literature I most often explored particular characters and used secondary sources to develop and support my interpretations of the text. These "other voices" were there to write with and against, and reading other writer's interpretations gave me a sense of authority in writing about my own theories. When writing pieces for my college paper, interviews and observation were my most common tools.

Several years later when I became a teacher, I began to fully recognize that research is part of being a writer of any kind not just because it adds to the writer's knowledge and thinking about a topic, or because that knowledge and the use of outside voices help the writer become an authority, but because research is interaction with other writers and thinkers. Good writing usually involves thinking, talking, and reading. Research is one way to be a part of that larger community of writers and thinkers.

I also realized that for my students to discover how research fit into their discipline and their interests—into their writing lives—I would have to work against the research paper as just another empty assignment. Writing teacher Ken Macrorie's *I-Search* was the first unconventional research project I undertook with my students. For this project writers pursue a question of their choice (such as "Who Invented Basketball?") and write about both the topic and the process they go through in researching and writing their papers. This project allows writers to approach the search in steps, beginning with what they already know or assume about the topic and building on that knowledge while examining the process of research. Because the story of the search is part of the research paper, there's room to talk (and write) about obstacles and successes writers encounter in using the library, using secondary sources, and writing about what they learned and how they gathered their information. The writer's thinking about the topic and about the new information they've collected is emphasized.

With Macrorie's *I-Search* paper you can chose a topic you care about, approach the research as an opportunity to learn, and abandon much of your anxiety at having to write a college research paper. The papers you learned to fear and loathe, as had I, are no longer the papers you are writing. What you are writing represents interesting and engaging explorations because you are interested and engaged in the topics and, therefore, in the research and the writing. The finding out about the topic and writing about the actual research and the results of the research becomes the focus. The details of research methodology and documentation become tools that are necessary to reach your goals for the projects.

Still, even the *I-Search* has a set pattern for the search, focuses heavily on a meta-analysis of the search, and doesn't address alternate methods of researching or alternate styles of writing. The purpose of the *I-Search* seems to be to create real research and acquaint writers with the methods, just as the traditional research paper seems designed to teach a standardized form. I want writers to discover that research has a purpose and a true place in their writing lives, and that the methods used for researching and writing are not the same for every project.

I thought it might be more challenging to consider projects without completely predetermining our ways of researching and writing. I knew there had to be some guidelines (say, requiring at least three sources as a minimum standard for writers to include), because researching means joining a community of researchers and communities do have rules to help create order out of chaos. But rules should be pushed to enhance learning and contribute new knowledge back to the community. So, I want writers to discover different ways of gathering information, which are more interactive than straight library work, and to experiment with untried ways of writing their drafts. I want writers to learn how it's normal and productive to use both alternate methods and alternate styles in the researching and writing of projects. Here's how this works.

These projects are different from conventional research papers in many ways. You are free to choose any topic—including abstract concepts such as love—and aren't required or expected to prove a hypothesis or even come to a certain conclusion. What you are expected to do as a writer-who-learns-as-a-researcher is to explore the topic and to complicate your thinking by reading, talking, observing, and writing. The interviews and field visits (described below) make your experience and knowledge as important as your textual sources. You are the authority on the subject, unlike conventional papers where you're tempted to borrow the authority of published writers. You are making your own interpretations and forming your own conclusions, rather than relying primarily on someone else's interpretations and conclusions.

The writing in the paper should reflect your topic, your experience with it, or create a mood or rhythm suitable to your information and purpose. Next, you have to determine the audiences for your paper. One writer in my class wrote a guide for fellow students planning to apply to medical schools. Another writer developed a travel guide for people wanting to travel in Europe as cheaply as possible. Since the audiences vary depending on the writers' purposes, the papers may or may not follow academic conventions.

It's important to write and talk about possible topics. Share ideas out loud and explore how you might narrow larger ideas and what local sources might be interesting. One writer, Jacky, writes in her self-evaluation, "When you said research project I was very disappointed. I was also put off because I couldn't really think of any thing that I was hot to research."

Jacky finally found a topic—new friendship—and began to compose her draft. She later writes, "When my fingers struck the keys, a research paper format didn't appear on the screen, but rather a story. Although it was not in typical form, it had all of the information that I had gathered and I was actually pleased with what I had written." Even though we talk about alternate style in class, many writers are nervous about breaking from the format that for them equals research. Jacky's group questioned her fictionlike approach because to them it didn't look like research. Jacky's paper opens like this:

> My legs buckled as my feet hit the earth and my knees were called to the rescue. The sky spread wide and murky above as the red clay splashed onto the cuffs of my jeans. The barking commands from the guard rang in my ears and the eight of us went to work.
> Indentured to the Leon County Work Program, we all reluctantly attended these ten-hour sessions of garbage collection. All of us from various walks of life and varying degrees of misdemeanors, yet bonded by the law.

She continues on to describe meeting two college students that day and the experiences that led to their friendship.

Throughout the writing Jacky describes the visual details, as well as her insights and fears about making new friends. She uses alternate style to include her thoughts along with dialogue with Nick and Jocelyn, and the points of common ground and points of extreme difference.

> "Hey, do you want to see pictures?"
> "Of course!"
> Faded rectangles of years past emerged in her hands. Nameless faces appeared, all with the same rounded build, prominent nose, and root beer hair like Jocelyn's. There was a tall, lanky man in one of the pictures cradling a woman in his arms.
> **************Biting wind and cold weather. Their backs turned from the camera, only the profiles of their faces, gazing at one another. The mountains, somewhere, with an old, paint-flaked barn in the background.*********************
> "This is my parents on their honeymoon. I love this picture because it shows how much they love each other."
> _____ Putrid envy raced through my blood, but I remained silent because I was awestruck by such a phenomenon as love between parents
> _____
> "My father and I were never very close,"
> _____ AH, A TOPIC THAT I COULD RELATE TO!!! _____ "until I came to FSU this year." Her face lit up.
> _____ OH, NEVERMIND. _____ "He and I write on the internet every day now . . ."
> The conversation laxed into more jovial topics and the night came to an

end. As I was walking home, I realized that Nick and Jocelyn led very different lives than I did and that I could learn a thing or two.

By the end of her paper, Jacky has traced the development of her friendship
with Jocelyn and Nick from their first meeting, through the insecurity of spending
time with new people, to several weeks later when their relationships were more
established.

Jacky easily moves away from the concept of the conventional research
paper by choosing an unconventional topic—how a friendship develops. She is
able to use interviews with Jocelyn and Nick and textual sources (a letter) to
explore something in her life that intrigues her. This paper is a good example
of alternate style in the methods Jacky uses to intersperse the dialogue with
what she's seeing and thinking. It also illustrates that writers don't need to stick
to the kinds of concrete questions that traditional research usually calls for.
Any topic can work when writers have an interest in it and can discover a purpose
and audience to pursue.

Just as Jacky's allowed herself to use a variety of writing techniques in a
research papers, the rest of this chapter provides ideas, suggestions, and practices that can lead you into a project that lets you research as a writer and to
explore alternative ways of presenting that research.

Getting Started as a Researcher

The first thing you need to know is that the research project is a chance for you
to explore something that is interesting to you. It might be a way to understand
an experience, learn more about skydiving before you jump out of the plane,
record family stories, find out about medical school before it's time to apply,
plan a trip to Europe, analyze your dream life, investigate the popularity of
soap operas, or contemplate love and friendship. Use the following prompts to
generate a list of possible topics.

1. a law/policy/rule that you don't understand
   (e.g., the Selective Service Draft or Affirmative Action)
2. a person (or group of people) you've never talked to before
   (e.g., a homeless woman or a priest)
3. something that frightens you
   (e.g., bats or the national deficit)
4. a club/major/activity on campus that you're curious about
   (e.g., the yoga club or a sorority)
5. something you've never tried before and want to try
   (e.g., hang gliding or African food)
6. something that makes you mad
   (e.g., underfunding in schools or plans to dump toxic wastes in the
   county)
7. anything else you want to know more about

Getting Focused

When you have a few ideas try a series of informal writings (try guided freewritings or other methods of brainstorming) to narrow down your choices. Then, take your top three choices and for each freewrite about

- why the topic is interesting to you
- what reason or purpose you would have in exploring it
- what you already know or think about the topic
- any previous experience you have with this topic
- questions you want to answer

Use these writings to choose the most interesting project. But before you make a final decision, consider what sources you could use to learn more about your possible topics.

Expanding Options

Unlike the conventional research paper that sends you to the library to find out what other people think about your topic, this assignment challenges you to discover what you think. What sources other than the library are available to you? Try to think of regional, state, community, or campus resources that allow you to observe, interview, or participate. Here are some source ideas to consider:

1. *Interviews:* Discuss your topic with a person who can share their relevant experiences, insight, education, or knowledge. Bring a list of specific questions you want to ask, and be prepared to think on your feet. You will need to take notes, or tape record this session (ask permission first) so that you can use direct quotations in your paper. Try to capture what they say and how they say it. If they speak in slang or don't use standard English, let the quotations reflect their unique use of language. Round out these notes by including physical descriptions and first impressions.

2. *Field Visit:* Go to a nearby place that is significant to your topic. Don't be afraid to make unexpected connections between a location and your topic. Pick a place that somehow contributes to your exploration. Take notes to record your observations, impressions, and sensual details (what you see, hear, smell, touch, taste).

3. *Your own experiences:* Consider writing about past experiences relevant to your topic. If it's safe and legal, you may want to take the opportunity to experience your topic firsthand (serving dinner at a homeless shelter, for instance).

4. *Textual Sources:* You may find these sources in the library or during the course of your interview and field visit. Texts include books, magazines, journals, pamphlets, charts, maps, pictures, drawings, . . . anything that is written by someone other than you. These "other voices" are there to join in the conversation about your topic.

Learning What You Learned

Just as there are many ways to gather the information for your research project, there are many ways to write about your discoveries. On your own, or in a group, make a list of all the rules you've been told about writing research papers (such as, every paragraph must have a thesis statement). You may find the rules deal mostly with the process of researching, the structure of the essay, documentation, and correct grammar and punctuation. Consider, or discuss, why these rules for conducting and writing research are used.

Some of the rules you list will be useful in writing your drafts. Documentation, for instance, allows you and the reader to see where the information came from. But breaking some rules (like never use "I") or creating new ones may lead to a better, more revealing draft. Choose a style that does more than give the information. Let the style reveal how you're approaching the topic or a mood you want the reader to feel. Explore your possibilities. Don't assume that the structure and style of the conventional research paper is the best way to share your new-found knowledge.

When Research Is for Writers, Writers Keep Researching

Research for personal projects—family history, genealogy, family stories, and biographies—may include

- gathering names and dates for a mini-genealogy
- recording the oral history of a grandparent (or other older family member)
- writing a biography of a relative who is no longer living using letters, newspaper clippings, and interviews with those who knew him or her
- using a social or historical perspective as a companion to events, locations, or people in your family
- investigating the history of your hometown and your family's history living there
- collecting favorite family recipes, and exploring the role of food in daily life, family celebrations, and religious holidays

What Other Writers Have Done

Like Jacky, other *writers choose to explore abstract topics,* which are not easy to define or quantify. Jessica writes about love by exploring what it means to different people in various circumstances, observing couples, and finally writing two stories about the same female character. In the first story, she is sixteen and her boyfriend has left for college after an unreconcilable fight. In the second story, the character is an adult, married with two children, looking back on her teenage experiences and reflecting what love means to her now in the context of being a wife and mother. She includes two pages of definitions of love that she had gathered in a survey.

Some *writers research information they need for travel or study plans.* They use the research project for their own needs, to answer real questions. For instance, Cara writes about traveling to Europe on a student's budget. Her final draft begins with an advertisement:

> CARA'S CHEAP CARAVAN—TRAVEL WITH THE GIRL WHO WROTE THE BOOK ON STICKING TO A TRAVEL BUDGET. NEVER AGAIN WILL YOU HAVE TO DEAL WITH SNOTTY TRAVEL AGENTS WHO ARE TRYING TO MAKE A BUCK AT YOUR EXPENSE. SEE THE REAL EUROPE, THE ONE PEOPLE WHO LIVE THERE KNOW AND LOVE. EXPERIENCE THE SELF-FULFILLMENT EARNED, AND THE KNOWLEDGE GAINED FROM VISITING NEW AND EXCITING PLACES! IT WILL BE AN ADVENTURE OF A LIFE TIME THAT YOU WILL NEVER FORGET!
>
> Ever since its establishment in 1995, Cara's travel service has assisted young travelers, like herself, who want to see the world, but at the same time have to do so on a conceivable budget. She too struggled with agencies who would not look for alternative lodging and transportation necessary for the frugal traveler. That is why she developed this service in order to fulfill other's dreams of traveling to Europe on their financial terms just as she did. Do not let the escalated price of traveling deter you any longer, call about one of our inexpensive excursion packets today and make your dreams a reality! CALL 1-800-CARAVAN.

After finishing the project she writes

> The research project proved to be very beneficial for me. I tried a new format in writing the final copy and I am slightly wary about whether or not it gets across all the information I wanted to. But, I could not make myself go through the boredom of creating your standard paper in which you simply spurt out statistics. BORING! I hope I can relate some of what I learned to you with the style I chose.

Another student, Steven, also chooses to research information he will need in the coming years. As a pre-med student, he wants to know what to do to prepare for medical school applications. His final draft, titled "From F.S.U. to Medical School: How to Get There," takes the form of an advising packet with a list of required course work, admissions test tips, the application process, and a timetable for planning.

Seth also researches his future by exploring the television production industry, the communications department, and looking for a summer internship. His paper, titled "What I Want To Do With My Life: A Research Project," begins by looking at his first interest in this area:

> When I graduated from high school I was constantly bombarded with the question: "So what are you going to do with your life?" I had certain ideas about where I wanted to be in the distant future, but the specifics were still a cloud of smoke. Throughout high school I changed "what I wanted to be" about as much as I changed my underwear (about once a week). I finally narrowed it down when I put together my first television show for my high school's television production class.

After completing the project he writes,

> Basically I thought the research paper was successful because I got a lot out of it. I feel better informed on the subject which is the whole point of it, right? I also had the opportunity to glimpse into the program that I am going to devote at least two years of my life to. . . . I am glad that you stressed the alternative format. I think it made for a better paper on my part, because I felt comfortable writing it. I found that my paper flows better in first person and it was nice to stray away from the normal, cold third person format of the usual research paper.

Many *writers choose adventurous topics*, like skydiving and bungee jumping. These are "fantasy" papers—exploring something they want to do but haven't yet tried. Most explore the possibilities from the ground, but one brave soul took the plunge. Of her jump, Kenia writes

> It was now our turn to jump, and I was in the group that was going to jump first. Dany, Jany, and I got ready to be strapped at the waist. I was to go in the middle. I felt so much safer this way. Having a person at each side, gave me a sense of protection. After we were tied, we were lifted up to the top of the crane. On the way up all I could say was "Oh my God." I waved to my friends who were watching us from the ground. I grabbed Dany's and Jany's hands, and held them up. And I told them, "Let's keep our hands up."
>
> When we reached the top, we were to stand on a platform. Then the guy who was up there counted down from five. Before I knew it, I had already jumped. I kept my eyes open, and my arms way up high above my head. I screamed all the way down. It seemed as if we were going to hit the ground, but before we reached the bottom, the cord swung forward, and we landed on a cushioned mat.
>
> I had so much fun, that if I would've had more money, I think I would've jumped again. I'm really glad everyone I went with had a good experience. No one chickened out, and no one threw up afterwards. That usually means everyone had fun.

We all have things we like better than other things, people, activities, objects, and so on. *Writers explore life-long interests* to gather more information, for a historical perspective, or to find out why others have the same obsession. In this example, Erica writes about her fascination with soap operas. A passage from her research paper reads

> I became a victim of soap operas when I was only a fetus in my mother's stomach. My mother in her younger years was an avid fan of All My Children, and so she planned that if I was a girl I would be named Erica after her favorite character Erica Kane. I guess you could say being named after a now infamous character has plunged me into the world of soaps as well. In the summer before the fourth grade, when I learned how my name came about, I was desperate to watch All My Children and see who this Erica Kane really was. I was captivated when I saw Erica Kane and all of the other characters on the show with their lavish wardrobes and stylish hair. Forbidden by my parents to watch soap operas because they thought I was too young, I would secretly sit in front of the TV and watch these "grown up" television shows. I became quite the manipulative girl at that age turning the channel from my soap opera to something a little more my own age when I would hear my mom calling. Since then I have become an avid soap fan. The many different characters with their romances, affairs, exploitations, heroic deeds and of course their good looks are one of the main reasons I have tuned into soap operas for so long.

Later she writes

> I pretty much enjoyed writing this paper. The only bad part was trying to figure out how to use the library but at least now I can find books there. This was an interesting paper for me to write since I watch soap operas myself. I learned about the history and I also learned how soaps affect different people.

Lindsay explores dreaming and the meaning of dreams through textual research and interviews where she asks people to share their dreams and what they think parts of the dream might mean.

Because she has been successful writing conventionally in high school, Lindsey finds it difficult to draft in alternate style. In her self-evaluation she writes,

> After I did my first draft, I tried and tried to think of a way to use the alternate styles. I read the paragraph on the "crot." Using this basic theme of the untransitional, unconnected, and unfitting paragraph, I mutated it into the style I came up with in my final draft. Instead of using paragraphs, I used short poems, and quotes from history that were unconnected to the text. I found this really successful in the paper. It also gave the paper a choppy, unflowing, and untraditional feeling. It put a sort of mystery in it, which is what my paper is all about, "the mystery of dreams."

Even later she writes,

> This project gave me the freedom to choose the topic that I wanted and was interested in, gather information in the way that I wanted to gather it, and

write the paper the way that I wanted to write it. This freedom has given me a lot of new research skills for future papers.

Writers regularly tackle social and political issues that troubled them. These are challenging papers to write and raise many questions and spark debate in response groups. In this case, Pete chooses to research Affirmative Action and address some of the questions he has about this policy. After completing his work, Pete writes,

> . . . [this] is a very complicated topic, but I enjoyed doing the research and thinking about my opinions. I discovered a lot about myself and my values. I learned that not everything has a clear cut answer to it. I talked to several people about the subject and found many opposing opinions.

In his paper, Pete explores the history of Affirmative Action, the reasons for its creation and the current debate over the usefulness and fairness of the policy.

Judy researches the Crazy Horse Memorial and in the process writes about prejudice toward Native Americans (including a rival football team that chanted "Bingo and Cigarettes" at FSU's football team mascot, Chief Osceola), and her own Uncle Bill, a full-blooded Cherokee. In her paper, she writes

> The most fascinating thing that Bill wants me to know is that he and the others on the reservation are not bitter to the white man. I'm not sure if that is true of all of the Cherokee people, or is it just the uniqueness of my Uncle Bill? He's happy because he has what he has always wanted . . . the land . . . and in its virgin form. I challenged him on the fact that I have been to Cherokee, North Carolina and left appalled at the way it has been "touristcized" with Indians in various beaded native dress sitting around performing "Indian" rituals . . . AND FOR $2.00 MORE, EVEN YOU CAN HAVE YOUR PICTURE TAKEN WITH A REAL INJUN CHIEF! *"Bingo and Cigarette . . . Cigarettes and Bingo. . . ."* Laughingly, Uncle Bill mentioned something about free enterprise . . . and isn't that the AMERICAN way?

Some of the writing you've just looked at may appear familiar, like personal essays or short fiction pieces. However, rarely are writers allowed to use the whole spectrum of writing techniques in research papers, which are considered by some to be an initiation into conventions. If that is their purpose, it implies that the work of a writer is adhering to strict rules even when they don't apply. However, a writer can—as you can—choose to research actively when assigned a conventional or unconventional research project at work or in school.

Work Cited

Macrorie, Ken. 1988. *The I-Search Paper.* Portsmouth, NH: Boynton/Cook.

II

Invitations to Risk-Taking, Play, and Radical Revision

7

It's Not Just Mumbo Jumbo
Taking Risks with Academic Writing

Elizabeth Rankin

> Ain't no rules if you don't break 'em
> Ain't no chances if you don't take 'em.
> —Guy Clark, *Picasso's Mandolin*

It's finals week and I'm reading through papers for my Twentieth Century Literature class. Aaron's paper comes in the form of a gray, sealed file envelope. Under the flap is written Aaron Glenn, English 407, Mumbo Jumbo File. It's not quite as odd as it sounds. Aaron isn't writing mumbo jumbo—he's writing about Ishmael Reed's 1971 novel of that title. And he knows I'm willing to read unusual papers. In this class, I have urged the students to find topics that really interest them, questions they want to pursue through writing. Here's part of what I said on the initial assignment sheet.

> It might be that thinking about your topic in this fashion leads you to write a fairly conventional paper. That's okay, as long as it's not just a mechanical paper. . . . But it might be that your paper looks very *un*conventional: incomplete, unpolished (at least in terms of thought or argument), full of questions and contradictions. As far as I'm concerned, that's okay too. In fact, that might be preferable in a course like this, in which there is no set material to convey and we're raising more questions than we're answering.

> Regardless of how you approach these papers, I hope you'll strive to make
> them genuine learning experiences. If I can see, when I read your paper, clear
> evidence of a mind at work on the page, I'll consider your paper successful.

The assignment is a little looser than I am used to giving. But that's because the course itself is an experiment for me. Its official title is Studies in
Twentieth Century Literature, but the subtitle is Texts We Want to Read Together.[1] Although normally the instructor chooses the texts for a lit course, I've
set this one up so that the students propose and present texts *they* want to read.
Aaron has chosen *Mumbo Jumbo*. It's a novel he has read before but finds
"impossible to understand" on a single reading. This class gives him a chance
to spend more time with it.

Despite my commitment to this open view of the course, however, I am
initially bewildered by Aaron's Mumbo Jumbo File. When I open it, the first
piece of writing I see is a photocopy of the preface to a scholarly book by a
prominent African American literary theorist. Scrawled across the top is this
handwritten note:

> Hey Sean,
>
> Ran across this by a guy named Henry Louis Gates, Jr. Think ya should take
> a look at it and think about bringing him in for some Q's.
> —Bob

Sean? Bob? What in the world is this? The next piece in the file is another
photocopied piece, this one titled "Miraculous Fiction Writers." Again there's
a scrawled note at the top:

> This is one of those essays by that Black I told ya about—Ishmael Reed
> —Get some guys on his ass!

By the time I get to the third piece—another short essay by Reed, another
handwritten note from Bob to Sean—I begin to see what Aaron is up to. This
is a paper on Reed's *Mumbo Jumbo* in the form of an FBI file on its "subver-
sive" author.

Once past my initial confusion, I read on with pleasure and delight. The
photocopied pieces, it turns out, are the only "conventional" academic materials in the file. In addition to fictional FBI agents, Aaron has created a fake
Dallas newspaper, with news stories, ads, and editorials pertaining to the events
and people of Reed's novel. He's also written a mock transcript of a Senate
hearing and a short segment of a Hollywood script based on that hearing, both
of which comment not only on the "meanings" of *Mumbo Jumbo* but also on
the whole idea of intertextuality—the notion that every written text, whether
poem or novel or academic essay or course syllabus, is made up of language
"borrowed" consciously or unconsciously from other texts, both written and
oral. Interwoven through all these imaginatively created documents are references to a wide range of ideas and events that show how deeply Aaron has

thought about the novel's social/cultural context. I'm impressed with how he brings in ideas from popular culture (the movie *Boyz in The Hood*), current affairs (the welfare debates), U.S. history (the 1950s McCarthy hearings), literary theory (Trilling, Eliot, Gates), and the work of other authors we read in this class (Zora Neal Hurston and Don DeLillo).

Clearly, Aaron has taken up the challenge I offered to the class. He has chosen to try something different, to boldly enter the literary arena, to bring imagination to bear on his critical work. It's worth noting, though, that despite its weirdness, Aaron's Mumbo Jumbo File accomplishes some of the same things as a standard research paper. For instance, the scholarly articles he's included are like quotations used to support a point—just bigger. And the information he offers in his "Dallas newspaper" article on Ishmael Reed gives standard background material on the author. Given these similarities, in fact, it isn't hard to imagine how the project might look in more traditional form. It would probably start with a quote from Henry Louis Gates' Preface to *The Signifying Monkey*, in which Gates talks about the importance of Reed's work. Then, to introduce Reed's ideas, there would be quotations from his own essays, "Miraculous Fiction" and "Black Irishman," followed by a thesis saying something about what Reed is up to in *Mumbo Jumbo*, how his novel works as a critique of American (and African American) literary and cultural traditions. It could have been a fine standard academic paper. Why didn't Aaron write it that way?

One reason, I'm sure, is that this was more fun. Look at it—Aaron is having a blast with this project! But the nontraditional form also allows Aaron to say some pretty complex things about the novel. For instance, in the Senate hearing transcript, a couple of Aaron's most important secondary sources get to "speak for themselves" in a way that points up the charged political context of their work. Could he have made that point in a more traditional paper? Perhaps— but not in such an effective way.

At the end of the file is a two-page, single-spaced "Note" in which Aaron explains what he has done in this very unconventional "paper" and gives his rationale for taking this approach. He writes:

> But am I not, through this file, putting words into Ishmael Reed's mouth? No more or no less than a paper written in a traditional style. In fact, I believe that my understanding of the material at hand is better conveyed through my writing of this Mumbo Jumbo File. In a more traditionally styled paper, especially a five page paper for this course in 20th Century Literature, it is very easy for students to simply fill those five or six pages with the words of other scholars. I could have easily written five pages on *Mumbo Jumbo* using what Henry Louis Gates writes in *The Signifying Monkey*. It in no way would mean that my understanding of *The Signifying Monkey* or *Mumbo Jumbo* was an understanding of quality. It would simply indicate that I was capable of regurgitating. . . .
>
> I hope that by my writing this and your reading this, that your mind's sprockets and cogs have begun to turn and grind. I hope that this has brought

to your attention the fact that much thought has been put into the creation of my Mumbo Jumbo File. Everything in the file, in my opinion, addresses *Mumbo Jumbo*. My file is meant to be funny, as *Mumbo Jumbo* often is. [But it also has very serious points to make, which Aaron elaborates on in his meta-commentary.] . . . I hope that you now feel compelled to examine every bit of my Mumbo Jumbo File and I hope that you do this because you enjoy it and not because you have to give me a grade.

Aaron needn't worry. I am fascinated with his Mumbo Jumbo File. Not only does it give me a rare behind-the-scenes look at what he has been reading and thinking and why he is so interested in Ishmael Reed, it also furthers *my* understanding of Reed's novel and the literary/cultural context it grows out of and responds to.

For Aaron, writing in this "alternative style" has allowed him to bring to his reading and writing the full range of his talents and capabilities. He hasn't had to leave anything out: not the literature and theory he knows, the jazz he loves, or the desktop publishing skills he has mastered. (I wish you could see that "newspaper" he produced—it's a piece of work!) As he writes, he's been able to call on what others have said in class, what he himself is thinking, and—perhaps most importantly—who he is as a reader and writer: a young white man from Minneapolis, a computer science major intrigued by African American literary and intellectual culture.

For me, reading Aaron's paper takes more time than I might usually spend, but it's very rewarding time. It demands that I step out of my too-familiar teacher role, that I bring *my* range of talents and capabilities to bear on the process of reading. That's pretty exciting. But it's also pretty scary. For one thing, I have to admit that I don't understand everything I read in Aaron's Mumbo Jumbo File. Paging through some of these imaginary documents, I hardly know what to think, much less how to comment. In fact, looking back at the file now, six months later, I'm embarrassed at how little I wrote in response. There are a few penciled comments in the margins—mostly questions, a few circled typos, but virtually nothing that would give Aaron a sense of how excited I am by his project, how much I have learned from it, how much I admire his work. Why not, I wonder? At the time, perhaps, I was simply stunned. Unable to draw on my usual repertoire of "teacherly" responses ("interesting thesis!" "good point," "transition could be smoother"), I just backed off and admired the effort. And maybe worried a little about what I "should" be saying.

Is that surprising—that teachers sometimes don't know what to say? (Or is it pretty apparent?) As a teacher, I'm disconcerted when I don't know how to respond to a student paper. (It must be how doctors feel when they encounter symptoms that throw them for a loop.) When I started teaching, this happened a lot. In fact, I still remember my first year of teaching, when I gave As to students whose papers, though mechanically correct, were . . . well . . . *boring*—so devoid of voice and significant content that I simply had no idea what to say to them. Later I would give such papers Cs, though I still wouldn't understand how to respond in a way that would help the writer improve. It wasn't until I had been teaching several years that I began to sense the fear of failure that lay behind those safe, correct but dull five-paragraph themes. These days, when I see papers like that, I usually know how I want to respond. Either I gently *invite* the writers out, try to get them working on projects they really care about, or I try to *jolt* them out, force them out of their safe cover and into a risk-taking mode where their writing can grow. In those earlier times, what helped me learn was simply experience. The more similar papers I saw, the more I began to learn how to deal with them. I think the same will happen as I invite more unconventional writing projects like those I got in Aaron's class. But in the meantime . . .

In the meantime, to be perfectly honest, I am still struggling with what to say about these unconventional papers. Usually, I try to be up front about my struggles, to think aloud in class (or in writing, as I'm doing here) about what my concerns are. Doing that isn't just being honest—it's also modeling the kind of thinking I expect my students to do: thinking that is sometimes "incomplete, unpolished, full of questions and contradictions," but also engaged, thoughtful, and unafraid to deal with complex ideas. As Aaron would say, it's thinking that "makes the mind's sprockets and cogs begin to grind."

Of course thinking like this can take many different forms, and not all of the successful projects in this class were as unconventional as Aaron's. Some were more like standard papers, with just a little added risk factor. For instance, Terry began his impressive technical analysis of Art Spiegelman's graphic novel *Maus* with a personal narrative about his life-long love affair with comics. Melinda combed through classmates' papers and came up with evidence of provocative gender differences in the way we talked about the books we read. And Kara reflected sensitively on family psychology as a theme in twentieth century literature, using her own family experiences as a backdrop for her consideration of course texts.

In several cases, although I liked what the students produced, I found I was uncertain about whether it was "academically sound" or "scholarly" enough. Was Chris's paper on *Death of a Salesman* a creative personal response to that play? Or was it only a powerful autobiographical essay about his parents' divorce? (And what do I mean by "only" in that sentence, anyway?) What about Max's meta-paper titled "This Is Not a Paper," and Rachel's wickedly funny parody of some of our livelier class discussions? Were these genuine attempts to draw together the work we had read and the things we had said about that work in class? Or were they simply clever evasions of the assignment—unconventional in style but lacking somehow in serious thought and substance?

I think I have some acquaintance with evasions like that. In fact, I think I've produced them! Back in the sixties, as an undergraduate English major, I took a class, the 18th Century Novel, from a particularly inventive teacher. One assignment in that class was to write a new chapter for the novel *Tristram Shandy*, a chapter that would show, through imitation, an understanding of and appreciation for the innovative formal aspects of that work. Twenty years later, as I assign such papers myself (there's a name for them now, ghost chapters) I think about the student I was and the paper I wrote. Painful as it is to admit, I was no Aaron.

What I mean by that is that I hadn't read as widely as Aaron has read, hadn't developed the passion he obviously has for his subject. For me, writing that ghost chapter for *Tristram Shandy* was fun, and my response was clever, but even at the time I knew I was evading the real challenge that had been offered me. I showed that I could imitate Sterne all right, but what I chose to imitate was simply a superficial aspect of his style—a chapter in which he inserts a blank page and asks the reader to imagine the scene he is too modest to report.

When I say my response evaded the real challenge of the assignment, I mean I knew at the time that I wasn't trying anything very difficult. All the complexity of Sterne's novel—his fascination with the intersection of fiction and reality, the ways we tell our stories and shape the narratives of our lives— I simply did not deal with. Probably because I was afraid I didn't understand.

That's one of the things I admire most about Aaron's Mumbo Jumbo File: it makes no claim to "understand" this complex novel, yet it is fearless in its willingness to try. In that respect, it is similar to another paper from the class, Rachel's take-off on Mark Leyner's satirical novel *Et Tu, Babe!*

Maybe it's because of my own evasions as a student that I was uneasy with Rachel's paper when I first encountered it. Titled Et Tu, Class!: A Short, Short, Short, Short Novel, the paper borrows Leyner's quick pace and his irreverent style, but while his book satirizes contemporary American culture, Rachel's paper satirizes our class. In it, Rachel herself is the central character, a new teacher put in charge of an uncontrollable class of mouthy kindergartners whose words and gestures are modeled so closely on those of people in our class that I would recognize them even if she hadn't used real first names. At one point, one of the most aggressive children, a passionate young Marxist named Kevin, "pulled out a 9mm pistol and shot off his teacher's left ear. 'That was so you'll never forget the significance of this day,' he said. 'I'm going to change the world, and I want you to be the first to know about it.'" In the Epilogue to Rachel's "novel," Kevin "has just been elected President of the United States . . . [He] has also just declared that all colors be banned, except for black and white, and has labeled the phrase 'just funny' as politically incorrect."

Although I laughed all the way through Rachel's satire (even at the part where I recognized myself), I was not sure how to evaluate it. What did this paper represent for Rachel? Was it an easy way out, a way to avoid serious engagement with the ideas we had raised in class? Or was I being too suspicious? After all, an easy way out for one person may be a meaningful experiment for another. After puzzling about this for a little while, I took a cue from Aaron's comments on his Mumbo Jumbo File and asked Rachel to write a commentary on her own work. Here's what she wrote.

> After we read *Et Tu, Babe* as a class, when we discussed it, people seemed to get down on Leyner pretty badly. [They said] that he is an egotistical pig, a pervert, and that he's vulgar and obscene, with nothing really to say in his writing. This bothered me, and that's when I started thinking about how I could write *Et Tu, Class*.
>
> I'll start off by saying that I'm not a gross, demented person, BUT it might seem that way from reading my paper. That is the first point I wanted to get across. A lot of times, writing does reflect on the author's personality, but it doesn't have to and we shouldn't automatically make assumptions. . . .
>
> Re-reading *Et Tu, Class*, I more and more think that we came up with a lot of questions, without leaving with many answers. That's okay, though. I'm not sure there are definite answers to our questions. I also realize that a lot of the time we would attack each other. . . . I felt scared to speak up most of the time (and took cover under the table) because I was afraid of getting shot down. Like what I'd have to say wouldn't be good enough or something. Maybe that's another reason I wrote this paper the way I did. I think I needed to "vent," as Jeanne [another classmate] would say.
>
> One more thing—why can't having fun be meaningful? We act like enjoying something that makes us laugh, or cry, or whatever, means nothing. We only think of "meaningful" [as] regarding to an increase of knowledge or something like that. Well, doesn't human emotion mean anything, even if it's a different kind of meaning? I think it's pretty damn important. The world would be a pretty sad place if people didn't know how to laugh at movies like Airplane, or didn't know even one good blonde joke.
>
> Libby, you're right. It was entertaining to write this paper, but I was thinking of more than "just laughing" as I wrote it. I hope you can sort of see what I'm thinking of in *Et Tu, Class*. I had a great time this semester!!

Reading Rachel's comments on her work, I feel she did learn something important. It might be quite different from what Aaron learned (more "process knowledge" than "content"), and it might not jibe as well with the traditional values of the university (which have more to do with cognitive "knowledge" than with affective "response"). But at the same time, I think Rachel is right: "meaning" is a pretty elusive concept, and it can reside in some unexpected places. In fact, when I think of it that way, that paper I wrote on *Tristram Shandy* may have had a powerful meaning for me. Why else would it stick in my mind so many years later, an example of one of the few times I really got to *play* with an assignment?

What I'm saying, I guess, is that *how* we write is sometimes as important as *what* we write. In exploring ways of writing that are undervalued in the university, or that may feel odd or different or not quite serious enough, we are keeping open as many channels of learning as possible. That can't be bad, can it?

It can be risky, though. Especially if you're focused on grades.

That's probably something I should have mentioned when I talked about my *Tristram Shandy* paper. I didn't get an A on that paper. But I don't think it was because I risked too much. It may have been because I didn't risk enough. In retrospect, I wish I had done what Aaron and Rachel did—used my writing as a way of exploring ideas that are interesting and complex and maybe even beyond total understanding. If I had risked more with that assignment, I would not only have had more fun with my writing, I would have learned more in the process. Still, I think I did learn one thing from that experience. I learned that I *could* take chances with my writing.

I hope you'll take some chances too.

Note

Thanks to all the students in my Fall, 1994 English 407 class for taking the risks that made this experiment successful—and special thanks to Aaron, Rachel, Ben, Terry, Melinda, Kara, and Max, whose work is mentioned or quoted in this essay. I wish I could use all your real names, but I promised you I wouldn't.

8

Grammar J, As in Jazzing Around
The Roles "Play" Plays in Style
Hans Ostrom

Play

I'm writing to share stuff with students who have adapted rather well to college writing, *thank-you-very-much*, but who may be a little bored by paper writing. I'm writing to share the same stuff with students who haven't adapted all the way—students who, when faced with writing a paper, feel dread, confusion, maybe a little anger or *acute* boredom. Also, I have a notion that, depending on what day it is, most students are members of both camps—the adapted and the unadapted.

Some of the stuff I have to share comes by way of Africa, perhaps to some a surprising source of ideas about writing. One teacher who read a draft of this essay asked, "Are you really writing to an audience like my class [at a big state college] of two African American students and the rest white?" I think this is a way of asking, "Will white kids get this?" It's not a question I expected, and that's a way of saying, "Any kids will get this." Well, maybe some African American students are immediately more interested in African stuff. Some aren't. Maybe some white kids are. Many aren't. Prior interest in Africa depends on individual interests, and in any case, "Africa" is not something we need to get hung up on here because . . .

. . . the key idea in this essay is **play**, which is the opposite of getting hung up on *anything*. What role does play play in your writing, what role should it play, how can it help you, regardless of (or, in addition to) **whatever** dread,

75

boredom, comfort, confusion, skill, and ethnicity you bring to your writing? I want to, and I want you to, play around with the idea of play-in-writing. Let me do a little set-up work first.

Who is Robert Farris Thompson, and how can he be of assistance?

Language Is Our Brains, So To Speak

Let's say **style is arrangement**.

Arrangement of *language* comes naturally to almost all human beings. Two important thinkers-about-language—American Noam Chomsky and Russian Mikhail Bakhtin—agree our brains are language and language is our brains. For Bakhtin, language is that material of which utterances (stuff we say and write) are made, stuff shaped by specific pressures exerted by persons, groups, economic structures, history, and the great-big mess that history is.

For Chomsky, utterances well up, as it were, from a deep, preexisting arrangement, a stratum, Universal Grammar. Water from a deep spring. He doesn't mean grammar as in grammar quizzes. He means something like How All Languages Hang Together, as well as Our In-Born Understanding of How Languages Hang Together. Think of this as a language hard-drive with which all human computers (brains) are equipped. (Ray Jackendoff has a good book that follows up on Chomsky's ideas. It's worth a look.)

We really aren't as different from one another as our utterances make us seem, it seems: the member of the British Parliament who speaks in ornate sentences and the American fourth grader speaking slang at a video arcade own the same basic language equipment. More: the seeming differences between us (let's say I say ain't and you don't) aren't true differences in the pure sense but artificial ones in the artificial sense. They are differences imposed for social or political reasons, not all that different from clothing fashions. A tuxedo, for instance, has certain status because people invest it with status, not because it's inherently "better" clothing than bluejeans. Let's say you are predisposed to exert your will over me or pretend to be better or smarter than I am; my saying ain't in certain situations feeds your predisposition, *even though you understand perfectly what I am saying to you*. ("Did you hear that guy say ain't at the party? What a bozo!") If a student walks on an American campus and, without irony or self-consciousness, says *ain't* or *mens*, how quickly that student is judged, pegged, pigeon-holed! Quickly? Heck, instantly. Ask yourself how you've judged someone or have been judged by someone based solely on the way you say a word or two.

A step further: reading and writing (R & W) are of this world of utterances about which I've been uttering. R & W branch from Language, from our In-Born Understanding of How Language Hangs Together. When such branches do not sprout or stop growing after they sprout, the reason in most cases is *social*. Of course, physical reasons are possible (a brain injury). But more likely, the circumstances of family, nation, class, gender, or some combination thereof prevent a particular "brain" (person) from acquiring and/or mastering R & W. The brain (the person) is in fine shape, linguistically speaking. It's just that a social obstruction of some sort is in the way. The brain (the person) is in need of guidance to get around the obstruction. Such guidance is also known as Teaching. Also known as Applied Generosity. Also known as Orientation—being welcomed, made to feel comfortable, not made to feel stupid, etc.

Who is Robert Farris Thompson, and how can he possibly help you write better?

The Concept of "Plerk"

And now for the notion of play-work, or *plerk*.

Most kindergarten teachers and foreign-language teachers and some Italian teachers-of-kids known as "the Ruggiero school" know children do not know the difference between work and play as they acquire a language, something that helps account for how efficiently they acquire a language. Children don't have time for such petty differences; they're too busy learning. Work and play are fused into work-and-play, more than the sum of the two parts. Plerk. If we're feeling stuffy today, we could use the word *facility*.

Hacky-sack, skateboarding, in-line skating, shooting hoops, pinball, throwing a pot (ceramics). I'm merely thinking of things I see students do where I teach. Help me out here and think of other things you do and do easily. Something that's plerk for you. Hold this example in mind, and as we move through the rest of this essay, keep comparing it/contrasting it to how you write.

Word up: As kids plerk at language, *word* is heard and played back and riffed and doubled and morphed. Think back to when you were six or seven. Or observe any five year old. Watch how much you and your friends play with language, make fun of weird language, mock the statements of your parents and other authorities and so forth. This is plerk. The Russian Bakhtin sometimes called this work-play "carnival." And aren't those conversations on the playground or in those late-night bull sessions in dorms like carnivals? Spontaneous performances of language?

This just in from our news desk: Children grow up.

But this clunker of a fact does not explain why plerk shrivels so rapidly in quasi-adult and adult (college) educational settings. Though in one sense college consists of little else EXCEPT writing, almost no one plays with writing. It's frequently grim work. With grim results. Mostly, college writing is a joyless affair. We might as well all dress as Puritans. (There's a reason, friends, why they call it the Protestant Work Ethic and not the Protestant Play Ethic.)

Who is Robert Farris Thompson, and can he lead us back to the Land of Plerk?

Big Issues Engulf Writing

To what extent do college teachers care what makes their students who they are? Do we give a damn? Do you give a damn? Do you care what makes teachers who we are? When teachers loathe students' writing, is it because they loathe students, loathe teaching, loathe their own writing? When students loathe writing, loathe the writing tasks they have been given, is it really because they're *bad* students, *lazy* students? And what about students to whom we give As but who nonetheless loathe writing—students who have learned to finesse the loathing? Are they the saddest cases of all? Okay, maybe *loathe* is too strong. Dread, boredom, confusion.

Often writing itself is not the issue. Often writing—students writing, students' writing—is a nexus for numerous impasses, big unresolved disagreements. Impasses in society, in academics. Such as: What is a college education for—the growth of the student, the health of the corporate world, neither, both? (To you this question's phrased *Why am I here?*) Such as: How often do you and your teachers actually move beyond a guessing game to reach some kind of intellectual agreement about the purposes of what's being written? How many teachers who are task masters of writing struggle desperately with their own writing demons, including the demon of writer's block? To what degree is writing, like standardized testing, one more way to categorize, "track," pigeonhole, and regulate the sheer masses of your students in this postindustrial society of ours? Writing, it seems to me, is almost too easy to use as a blank screen on which to project impasses of personal, social, and institutional kinds. The notion of play (plerk) opens up some paths around the impasses. *Ladies and gentlemen, Mr. Robert Farris Thompson . . .*

A Different Philosophy of Art and Writing and Style

Out of Africa, courtesy of Mr. Thompson, a "Philosophy of discourse." Let's say for the moment it means "the big picture"—a culture's deep sense of how talking, listening, writing, reading (discourse) functions—operates, works, plays. A culture's deep sense of how things, including writing, are *arranged*, and remember, we said *style is arrangement.*

Let me play some selections (not sold in stores!), with my brief comments in brackets, to help us get what we need to get out of this "Africa stuff." What I need you to do in the next page or so is use that example of plerk (hacky-sack, pinball, whatever *thing you do easily*) and notice how it's also an example of what our guy Thompson's getting at, and then the next step's to see how the stuff might work/does work/can work in writing. Your writing.

The first quotation's a little textbooky, but just go with it for the moment:

> *Flash of the Spirit* is about visual and philosophic streams of creativity and imagination, running parallel to the massive musical and choreographic mo-

dalities that connect black persons of the western hemisphere. . . . Among those [organizing] principles are the *dominance of a percussive performance style . . ., a propensity for multiple meter . . ., overlapping call and response . . ., inner pulse control . . ., offbeat phrasing . . ., [and] songs and dances of social allusion.* (Thompson, xiii)

[Some more big terms here, I know. But don't worry. "Dominance of percussive performance style" means, for example, *heavy on the drums*. Think of Cuban music, salsa music, earthier forms of jazz and rock and roll, rock-a-billy, rap and hip hop. Thompson's basically just giving labels to elements in music that are found from Kenya to Cuba, from Chicago to Buenos Aires. PLEASE note that such elements have spread beyond music into all areas of culture produced by persons of all ethnic backgrounds.

Just look at an MTV video—of the group Salt'N Peppa, let's say, or one like it. Heavy on the beat. Overlapping voices—conversations within the song. Perhaps a couple of meters (set rhythms) overlap. And "social allusion"—references to (in this case) urban life, to predicaments some young black women face, to social problems. This is basically what Thompson's talking about, and, **no**, it doesn't have to be rap music, so don't get hung up on that.]

The Yoruba religion, the worship of various spirits under God, presents a lim-

Generosity, the highest form of morality in Yoruba traditional terms . . . (Thompson, 13)

[Consider how *un*generous, ungiving, some supposedly moral people are. Consider how big a role punishment and retribution (taking, not giving) play in the moral scheme of some people. Consider how fiercely some teachers seem to attack the writing of their students, as if they (the teachers) were at some level "morally outraged." *Consider how much you yourself may punish yourself as you write, how much you've internalized the unforgiving nature of criticism you've received.*]

The Yoruba religion, the worship of various spirits under God, presents a limitless horizon of vivid moral beings, generous yet intimidating. They are messengers and embodiments of *ashe*, spiritual command, the power-to-make-things-happen, God's own enabling light rendered accessible to men and women. (Thompson, 5)

[Don't worry. No one's advising a conversion to Yoruba religion—though a smart-alecky voice in me says, "It couldn't hurt!" In this quotation, it's more important to concentrate on the idea of *ashe*. Consider when something has come really easily to you—in writing, sports, music, art—that example you're carrying from earlier in this essay. Whatever you're doing just seems to happen and happen well, as if (a paradox) you were in complete control but had no need to control the flow of the thing. This is a kind of *ashe*. It's a power. It's not necessarily a gift, though. It can come from practice—from "plerking" at in-line skating, for instance, from writing comfortably in a journal or on a draft.]

> I refer to the cone-on-cylinder as a multihabitational unit instead of a house. It is not merely an architectural structure but a representation of the individual within his or her social universe. (Eddy, 27)

[Wow, there's a quotation out of left field. But consider how all people, but especially kids, *make rooms their own*, how the room—the living space—is a fusion of shelter and art, the practical and the emotional. Consider the power of such places. There is a force—*ashe*—in a teenager's room, like that of a magical cave. This person Eddy is thinking about such force, except in the context of certain African homes. How does this cone-cylinder deal apply to your writing? Well, a paper is like a house—it is practical and personal, work and play, directed to a teacher and others but also springing from within. Also, chiefly through writing, you make an intellectual space for yourself in a course, at a college. You impose yourself. Writing comes easiest to you and me when the writing process fuses the practical and the personal. If we are totally practical, working on that paper like a robot, we come up with a robot paper, complete with robot thesis. If we're totally personal, we probably won't connect with whomever is reading the thing.]

Of Kentucky folk-sculptor Henry Dorsey

> Dedicating himself to work that was play, to labor that was festive, displaying his art in a communal round, Dorsey rescued objects thrown away by persons trained to see only single functions in them, recycling them in a deeper sense. (Thompson, 158)

[Dorsey took the discarded stuff around him—everything from wheel hubs to tin cans—and turned them into amazing sculpture. When we read and write, sez me, we can often see only single functions—in words, terms, concepts, even in formats (term paper, lab report, critical analysis); consequently, we often write with a kind of bored fatigue, going through the motions, picking up tin cans, throwing them in the garbage. When we find a way to make the language our own, we see multiple functions. We have room to move. The big ol' heavy term from the psychology textbook suddenly works for us in a different way; we're able to lift it, we bring it into our sense of language, use it as we see it. We cast off bored fatigue and write potently, just as Dorsey sculpted powerfully with material other people regarded as clumsy nonartistic material.]

So: the big picture here is that historian Robert Farris Thompson's work, itself a massive reconsideration of African philosophies and discourse, unexpectedly gives us a way out of our frequently grim, joyless, viciously circular, alienated zones of writing. More specifically, here's how Thompson does this:

1. As the reference to Henry Dorsey suggests, many of the African philosophies of text, visual art, textiles, music, and dance heal *the rift between work and play*. The effects of this fusion are astounding—witness the presence of blues, jazz, rhythmized textiles, etc. across U.S. culture. More

to the point, the effects dovetail with the Bakhtinian and Chomskyan ideas mentioned above (the Universal Grammar stuff); that is, they are more applicable than many of the Western philosophical ideas (including ones from Descartes and Locke, but this is just an aside) that have influenced our thinking about writing. *In the culture of college writing, there's a chasm between work and play*: That's an idea I want you to consider, and I know you can think of examples of this chasm from your own experience, as I know my students can.

2. *Improvisation.* Call and response. Off-beatedness—a deliberate, built-in, serious-and-playful irreverence toward received form. Collaboration. Fusion of the personal and the social. A recognition of the *ashe* (power to make things happen) in everyone. We all have It—*the power to make linguistic things happen.* (Earlier here we called it Universal Grammar.) I see it and my students see it when their writing goes well. And now that I think about it, I also see it in the way you—students—dress, mixing and matching stuff at will, playing riffs with the stuff you pull off the rack—or off your floor.

3. What drives these African views seem remarkably *postmodern*—this computerized, saturated-with-info, glutted, full-of-stuff, cross-cultural-wired, whacked-out world of ours. Funny, but as old as some of the African ideas are, they *know what to do with chaos and fragmentation and information overload;* they are not afraid of these things; improvisation and the "deep recycling" of Henry Dorsey's folk sculpture look at chaos and fragmentation, even alleged junk, as sources of energy, not threats to coherence.

One could argue that cyberspace is a culmination of Anglo-European technological culture, but one could also argue that what Thompson calls the African "flash of the spirit" was ready all along for the hyperflexibility and superabundance of cyberspace. In the age of the internet and cyberspace, channel-surfing, and changing careers nine times in a lifetime, such views may be as useful as water on a desert hike.

Whatever we might think of the five-paragraph essay and its cousins, are they supple enough to thrive in the age of discourse in which we find ourselves? Even if the internet and cyberspace and other weirdnesses of modern life did not exist, college *itself* would still be fragmented. How strange and potentially wonderful but nonetheless fragmented it is to attend a politics class at 11:00, eat lunch in a cafeteria, conduct a biology experiment at 1:00, and start drafting an anthro paper at 5:00—after lacrosse practice. The scheduling gives it all a veneer of logic, but from another angle it's surreal; so, on every campus there's a need for flexibility and play as you write your politics and biology papers, write a computer program, write a job application—all in the course of a day. Play is not incidental but vital.

You're Not Here

Oh, I **do** wish you were here, in my office, foggy day in the Pacific Northwest, a big fir tree outside the window of my pig-sty office (speaking of cylindrical houses and other weird spaces). Wish you were here to talk about specific things you've written, are writing. Writing that's gone well and not gone well. How as writers you've adapted and not adapted. And we could banter and mumble about **rhythm, contest, collaboration**, and **possession**—and **plerk**. But you're not here, and by this time I'm someplace else, too. So the fall-back position is for you to talk back to the next few paragraphs, bring them into your own workshop of ideas, strip them for parts, reassemble them according to writing you're doing right now, according to what kind of writer you think you are today.

Rhythm

Whether we're talking first-year writing, sociology, bio-lab reports, memos, or graffiti, language exists in time and is a timed thing—*rhythmed*. At some point in all classes, you should play with the rhythms of whatever you're asked to write, getting at least elbow deep into the movement of the text. If, for example, your sociology text seems somehow leaden, writing in the rhythms of that sociology text can at least make the text more familiar. I'm calling for something more than imitation and something less than (or different from) parody. An Elvis *impersonation* as opposed to an Elvis *impression*! I'm calling for something as simple as rewriting and jazzing-around-with a particularly sociologistic sociology sentence, a real Max Weber humdingerism. You should be invited into such a sentence before you are asked to understand it. Invite yourself. Crash the party of expert language.

Moreover, in this video-saturated culture, don't you think you oughtta be editing your own videos, should "write" videos instead of and/or in addition to papers? "Mike and I have a video due tomorrow" should be heard as often as "I have a poli-sci paper due tomorrow." What are the rhythms of this video-computer-culture, and why aren't you writing and rewriting those rhythms? It's crazy not to. It can be as simple as proposing experimental projects in place of traditional ones.

And of course writing-as-a-process, the act of writing, is a timed thing, too. A classic college-lore example is of the person who waits till 2 A.M. the morning before a big paper's due to start on the paper. This is like starting a song at the end of the song, the rhythm of the writing process wrecked. More usefully, just look at the larger rhythms of your own writing act sometimes. How could you smooth them out, synchronize, or syncopate them differently? What are the parts and are the parts moving well together? There's a rhythm to work days and vacation days. There's a rhythm within that unit/those units of time in which you write.

Contest

What is written in college should be contested. You and your teachers should yammer and jabber about assignments with playful but serious irreverence. Negotiate. Both sides should be willing to take as much as they give. You should (in a perfect world!) always feel free to ask why you're being ask to write what they write, and teachers should feel free to jettison old assignments—or to stick by them, IF they seem relevant to the plerk of learning. But the web of each class should include strands of contesting, flexible power negotiations, contested, and improvised "papers." Obviously, you shouldn't bang your heads against the brick wall of obstinate professors, especially if your grade depends on it. But if you see opportunities to negotiate, seize 'em. Be a player.

Collaboration

We know about this, don't we? Peer review, workgroups, and such. But take it further. Students should *play off* of one another's papers, cowrite, corevise, revise professors' prose, codesign paper topics. "But what does this do to our concepts of plagiarism and our systems of grading?" Exactly. I'm not encouraging plagiarism or academic dishonesty, but I am encouraging you/us to question how you/we define "authorship." And look at the so-called Real World. *Ensemble writing is the rule, not the exception.* Scientists, lawyers, judges, textbook writers, insurance adjusters, business persons, politicos, film writers—it's all ensemble writing! There are no singly authored annual reports or legal briefs or political speeches! The Declaration of Independence was not independently written! The Constitution was a group presentation! The internet and cyberspace have only accelerated the process to the speed of light. Why do we cling so desperately to the old ox cart of single authorship? I'm not saying banish the singly authored paper; I'm just saying, "Get real," and after getting real, use the reality of ensemble writing as an opportunity and an occasion, a mode of pedagogy.

Possession: A sporting idea

It's your play, the ball is in your court, change of possession. As hinted at by **contest** and **collaboration** above, you need to own the writing you do, just as you "own" your personal example of plerk (pinball? sailboarding? ceramics?). I'm convinced, after twelve years in the thick of all sorts of college writing, that much so-called bad student writing springs from lack of ownership. Even after you've completed a paper and the writing's gone fairly well, aren't there times when the finished product seems to belong more to the professor than to you?

Do whatever you can to own the things you write, to make "assignments" your own, just as an actor takes a role and runs with it. If the assignment looks and feels like a stupid tin can, look at it from a different angle, the way folk-sculptor Henry Dorsey would.

Possession also means possessing the language. When Dorsey picked up a fan belt or a roll of wire, he possessed it, made it his, redefined its function and meaning, recycled it into *his* (and his culture's) vision and visual text, re-presented it to the world—surprise! When you buy a flannel shirt, you make it *your* flannel shirt by rolling up the sleeves, by what you wear it with, by spill-ing paint on it, etc. You similarly need to possess the language of disciplines and courses, make it your own, drink it in, reshape it. Hence the need for rhythm-play, contesting, collaboration, too.

Play as in Big Style

The Buddhists speak of Big Mind. We need to think of Big Style, a way of seeing ourselves and our writing wholly. Instead we often still think of style as a series of small, surgical, "tasteful" word choices and authorial dance steps. Strunk and White's *Elements of Style* is the wildly famous bible of such sur-gery. Take a gander at page 70, though, where Strunk and White advise, 1. *Place yourself in the background. 2. Write in a way that comes naturally."* Um, what if the way that comes naturally is to put myself in the foreground? [Um] what if my teacher, who after all is THE reader, wants me and the pronoun *I* in the foreground? [Um] my friend got an A on her philosophy paper, but I read it and it didn't seem "naturally" to me.

[Hey] *The Elements of Style* is a sharp little book with some interesting advice, but it sprouts up from the loam of an unacknowledged Big Style—middle-class New England, where terseness and understatement are a way that comes naturally, where *The New Yorker* is the talk of that particular town. The book is the elements of *A* style. Maybe in some cases the precise writing sur-gery it advocates is useful; probably in other cases it isn't. What I'm saying is, let's acknowledge the Big Styles behind the little styles we advocate, and let's look around for other Big Styles. What I'm saying is, always ask questions about the Big Style in which you're asked to write papers. How did the style come into being? What do you like and not like about it? "Pay no attention to the man behind the curtain," says the alleged Wizard of Oz. Big Style is the person behind the curtain. Ask teachers to talk about this style, about what they see as its purpose, its strengths and weaknesses. Ask, in a nice way, what's behind the curtain.

Wayne and Jonathan and You

In an essay like this it's tempting to reprint chunks of students' essays or a whole essay as An Example, but I want to resist the temptation because I really want you to turn to your own writing and writing practices, and a lot of what we're kicking around here has to do with avoiding templates and formulas and elements of strunks, has to do with personal, specific playings-out of Grammar-J-Jazzing-Around, has to do with picking up the instrument—your own writing—and playing, performing your own writing, as it were and as it is. On the other hand, knowing how much some readers like An Example, I'll compromise and give a couple anecdotes about Wayne and Jonathan, but it's the maneuvers the two made—not so much their actual papers—that are key.

Wayne: a couple of weeks into the course, he let it be known he had to earn an A because his parents demanded it. His attitude toward writing was grim and joyless, and my not-so-grim-and-joyless attitude toward teaching and writing only made him more grim. Why? Because "the rules" had changed. I wasn't the sort of English teacher he expected. He wanted a formula for what I expected. Instead, he found himself in a classroom culture that invented itself. Often I'd ask the class what was on their minds; they'd find a subject; I'd incite them to argue and cavort. Out of this Petri dish of opinion, outrage, laughter, and debate would come a subject sometimes. Wayne didn't like this—the class determining the subject, the sense that paper topics and paper shapes were negotiable, the sense that things were in flux, everything from audience and purpose to what might happen in the next class session. He didn't really go for peer review of drafts either. He saw himself as a lone wolf, competing in college by and for himself. This was how he had learned to thrive in high school.

Not intending to, I began one session by asking about drugs on campus. A good twenty years away from my own undergraduate experience, I just found myself curious that morning about who ingested what and why these days. Much to my surprise, and to the hilarity of everyone in the room, tales sprang up of rather widespread mushroom use. Little bands of students apparently roamed the football field at night; football fields in the Pacific Northwest grow mushrooms. The discussion ranged from there to less comic topics—self-destructiveness, students dropping out, the contrast between the public-relations image of colleges and the reality of Generation X. The discussions seemed so rich I said we should probably write about "drugs on campus." Then I said I wanted to throw at them a deliberately awkward essay format—a "report" that would break abruptly in two parts. In part one, they would give their assessment of the drug problem or situation on campus. In part two, they would offer recommendations or observations. I told them it was a "findings and recommendations" format that one often had to wrestle with in all sorts of jobs. I wanted them to wrestle with it, find a way to make it work for them, get inside it. Combining the energy of the discussion with the deenergizing format was an experiment in writer's alienation I wanted us to go through. The class wasn't thrilled, but they understood the experiment and *took possession of it* from an experimental point of view. We *negotiated* from there.

Wayne broke through. He repositioned himself from Dutiful Son and Academic Lone Wolf to—well, to Wayne, a living, breathing citizen of *that* particular writing culture. This is how his essay began:

"This is your university. This is your university on drugs."

Marvelous. Playful. Playing a riff on the famous fried-egg commercial. (Remember Mr. Thompson's phrase, *"songs and dances of social allusion*?)" Playing with language. Playing with a key idea that came up in the discussion—the contrast between public relations and campus reality. Hinting at the combination of comedy (student roaming the football field pretending NOT to be looking for mushrooms) and tragedy (dropping out, stoned and lost) of drug use. His essay took off from that smooth runway and touched down several wonderful pages later. Wonderful mainly *for Wayne* (forget my reader's pleasure) who fused work and play, found the power to make things happen, spoke his mind, who played off the class discussion, wove together strands of language from many sources—television, campus talk, standard English, Hawaiian slang. Style! Wayne's style. The larger style of the classroom culture. Style as the particular class in a particular course with particular things to write and words moving through time across the page, across drafts and computer screens, across Wayne's life as Wayne's life moved across the life of his parents, across the life of "an education." Movement, work, play; off the beat and on the beat; calling out a subject and responding to it, responding to others who call out their opinions and outrages.

By shifting his stance just a little, Wayne shed that boredom, dread, and/ or fatigue most students feel, that thing I talked about at the beginning. He took a line from a TV commercial, something most people would deem inappropriate for a college paper, and like the sculptor Henry Dorsey, he *made* it appropriate. He turned it into a thesis, for heaven's sake! Do you see the move Wayne made, how the move was rooted in lots of stuff happening in class and with Wayne before "the paper" was ever an issue? Wayne—finding a way to **possess** the paper. Giving himself a chance **to make things happen** there in the first sentence of his paper. Being **generous** to himself, giving *himself* a break from the grim work of writing. Taking a television line and playing it back in a different song altogether. Turning writing into plerk.

And no, I'm not saying that everything should be a riff or a joke. In the same class, a student I'll call Jonathan wrote a paper about the film *Come See the Paradise*, which is set against the backdrop of the internment of Japanese Americans during World War II. Here is a sentence from his first paragraph: "The synopsis of the movie on the back of the laser-disc jacket alludes to the fact that the main focus of the story is not the injustices of the internment or the hardships endured, but the attempt of Jack to gain the acceptance of Lilly's family." This is more of an academic sentence, yes? There are ways to make it smoother, to play with it. But I liked it a lot. It's a real sentence, written with authority. It begins to crack open this movie for us—can you feel that happening, even if you haven't seen the film? I like the way Jonathan demystified the assignment and talked about the concrete reality of looking at the jacket of the laser disc; and, I liked how he used this concrete fact as a step to his thesis, which is that romance in the movie obscures some vital history. In his own way, not Wayne's flashier way, Jonathan made that particular assignment his own. Picking up the dust jacket, looking at it not as a dust jacket but a way to get to his essay's main point (think of folk-sculptor Henry Dorsey)—this, too, is a form of plerk, improvisation, and possession. His playing with the conventions of an opening paragraph is more serious, more academic, let's say. But it is still play in the sense of making the writing his own. Plerk. It is still Grammar J, let's say—**contest, rhythm, collaboration, work-play, improvisation, possession**. Make it *your* grammar j.

Works Cited

Bakhtin, Mikhail. 1986. *Speech Genres and Other Late Essays*. trans. Vern W. McGee. Austin, TX: U of Texas P.

Chomsky, Noam. 1968. *Language and Mind*. New York, NY: Harcourt, Brace & World.

Chomsky, Noam. 1975. *Reflections on Language*. New York, NY: Pantheon.

Eddy, Tod. Spring, 1974. "Manding Architecture From Africa to the New World: A Study in the History of African and Afro-Mexican Art." Unpublished paper. Cited in Thompson.

Edwards, Carolyn, Lella Gandini, and George Forman. 1993. *The Hundred Languages of Children: The Reggio Emilia Approach to Early Childhood Education*. Norwood, NJ: Ablex.

Jackendoff, Ray. 1994. *Patterns in the Mind: Language and Human Nature*. New York, NY: Basic Books.

Strunk, William, Jr. and E.B. White. 1979. *The Elements of Style*. 3rd Ed. New York, NY: Macmillan.

Thompson, Robert Farris. 1984. *Flash of the Spirit*. New York, NY: Vintage.

9

Distorting the Mirror
Radical Revision and Writers' Shifting Perspectives

Kim Haimes Korn

Meanings are not prebaked or set for all time; they are created,
found, formed, and reformed.

Ann E. Berthoff, *The Making of
Meaning* (70)

Revision as Invention

As Berthoff suggests, meaning for writers comes about through the acts of
forming and reforming and when revision is seen as an act of invention rather
than editing. Similarly, style in the writing classroom is often considered in
terms of arrangement, voice, and effect and the ways we shape our texts for
others. These audience considerations are obviously important, but alternate
style shifts can be seen as a way of using writing to think and learn. As we've
seen through other works in this collection, alternate styles involve teachers
and students in taking risks in thinking, reading, and writing. Like writing to
think, learn, or discover, it is uncertainty that makes experimentation in alternate style a valuable process of meaning-making for writers. My experience as
a writer, a student, and a teacher has helped me understand that my most valuable insights occur in times of chaos or ambiguity which are, as I.A. Richards
states, the "hinges of thought." Since it is only natural that we gravitate towards

situations that are familiar and resist surrendering control, it is important to find strategies that encourage us to step out of our writing comfort zones. Style shifts can give us insight, help us see, resee, enlarge, and productively distort our ideas or maybe even change our perspectives.

It is with this in mind that I brought the concept of style shifts into my writing classroom, which is the result of many collaborative conversations with other teachers and students of writing. I have tried to support a classroom environment that is open to experimental texts and have encouraged students to explore alternate genre options of fiction, dialogue, and poetry in place of expository essays. *Radical revision*, a term passed on to me by Wendy Bishop, is an extension on this idea that asks us as writers to move out of our comfort zones and revise our writings in ways that challenge us to make the familiar strange (see her "Risk Taking and Radical Revision"). In order to write a radical revision it is necessary to define the term *radical* for ourselves, which requires both an analysis of our tried and true habits as writers and a willingness to let them go. This revision process facilitates a close, conscious look at the choices we, as writers, make in relation to both form and content.

In my composition classes, for at least one of the assignments, I ask students to revise a paper in such a way that they use ideas from one of their earlier essays but rewrite the paper so there is a shift in style, content, or format. I give them suggestions about shifts in genre, perspective, voice, emphasis, but also encourage them to think of some of their own.

As long as I have included radical revision in my classes I have been continuously in awe of the variety of insightful ways students undertake the assignment. To name a few, one student addressed the assignment by changing her expository essay into a collection of letters, another changed the point of view from a personal narrative to the perspective of an outside observer, while still another changed the emphasis of her ideas by enlarging a portion of her essay that was insignificant in the first draft. Although this assignment is often initially met with resistance, I found that when given the opportunity (which is often interpreted as "permission") writers find creative ways to struggle with the relationship between content and form.

Although this might sound like a daunting task, it is important to understand that, as Bishop states, "There is no real risk-taking without the possibility of failure." Sometimes the writings work and sometimes they flop, but they always involve us as writers in different sorts of thinking processes, which I believe broadens our perspectives.

What follows is my own radical revision of one student's response to this assignment. I created a collage or patchwork quilt (one of the revision possibilities I give my students) which is drawn from conferences (set in italics), group discussions (set as dialogue), teacher's assignment (set in brackets), and student writing (set in bold) (underlined material is radical revision draft), created by my student, Tiffany, during the course of a first-year writing class:

Distorting the Mirror

In my high school english class we never did nothing. The teacher would tell us to just talk. Just socialize. We didn't do anything. She might give us a vocabulary paper with 10 words. That is how we got our grade. We were all like, 'Why don't we ever do anything in here?' I mean, we didn't like it because what can you talk about for a whole year? That much excitement doesn't go on in high school.

At our high school reunion we will want to know how many people got killed. We'll go to see who is still living.

I'll always have a trade to fall back on.

I want a chance for me to say something and have people actually listen.

The teacher is always right.

The audience can't really say anything because they don't really know about you. They probably know as much as you do.

Tiffany: I notice that a lot of guys like cartoons.

Latisha: They love it man.

Tiffany: My cousins are like 22 years old and they jump up at 8:00 in the morning. Oh, X-man is coming on. They turn on the TV and I am like, let me get out of here because I don't watch cartoons.

Kim: I never thought about it being only a male thing.

Tiffany: Yeah, they play video games until they get about 50. No, I don't like cartoons or games.

Latisha: I agree with you. I don't like them.

Romeo: Come on girls. I like them.

Tiffany: You would think as guys got older they would grow out of stuff like that.

Romeo: Are you kidding? We never grow up.

Tiffany: OK you go to the mall shopping and there they are in the video store. I gotta buy me a cartridge, I gotta buy a cartridge for the game. I am not going to spend no $60 on a game. I could buy me a pair of tennis shoes.

These are my ideas, so they can't be wrong.

To me, something on paper is hard to get. It has always been hard for me to comprehend something right off of paper. I need to hear it and if someone is talking to me I will pick it right up.

[Radical Revision entails not only an extension and refinement of your ideas but also a shift in the paper's style, content, or format.]

I wrote my paper the way I wanted it the first time.

[This assignment is meant to challenge you by causing you to look at something familiar in a radically different way and to give you a chance to experiment with different types of writing.]

Just tell me what you want and I will do it.

[Consider changing genres, perspectives, voice, emphasis, form.]

When I was younger I had a very bad attitude. My attitude was bad because I never listened to anyone. I never did what anyone told me to do without being nasty about it. I always snapped when someone tried to tell me what was good for me (even though it was good for me), I was always stubborn. I gave all my teachers, counselors, and deans a hard time by being very nasty towards them and by telling them they don't tell me what to do. I don't care if they called my mother and told her what I did and on one occasion I told one of my teachers to go to hell.

When my baby was younger she had a very bad attitude. I don't know where she inherited that attitude from because she didn't get it from me or her father. I sometimes wonder if Tiffany picked up that bad habit from her older cousin who often babysat her when I went to work. She sometimes lets her attitude overpower her and portrayed like she was a demon. As a mother I often feared about my daughter's well being where ever she was. Tiffany was a child who always spoke negatively towards others no matter who they were or what kind of authority they had. I found myself making many visits to her school dealing with incidents involving her attitude. I often wondered how everybody that knew her put up with her attitude. I could barely put up with her attitude but I said that I had to cope with it because I was the only person who was going to try to change her and make her a better person.

The things that made the difference in my attitude was my mother constantly talking to me about it and realizing that I was getting older and should be getting wiser and that I really had no reason to have a bad attitude with people.

We often had long conversations regarding her attitude but Tiffany never paid me any attention because she really didn't want to hear what I had to say because she felt that she already knew what I was going to tell her. Tiffany never realized that she couldn't live her life with such a bad attitude until she got older. She started listening to me when she noticed that everything I tried to tell her was true and that I was not trying to be mean to her.

The radical revision is really what had me pissed off because I said, "Why does it matter to think about it from someone else's point-of-view because I always seem to think that my point of view is right. But I realized after I wrote this paper that I was wrong. I was proud to know that I could write a paper from my mother's point of view.

The topic about my mother and myself is the writing that I found to have the greatest importance to me because in this paper I reflected back on my child-

*hood and it helped me see how much I have changed as a person. I noticed
what kind of problems I caused in my mothers life.*

*All the comments on my paper were things I hadn't really thought about before.
Every comment that they make I will like read my paper and I think that could
fit in right here or I can come back and look at it all again.*

*With these assignments I say to myself, "Why do we have to keep doing this
revision?" But when you read the first paper and read the last paper it is like
a big difference. Everybody commented and it opened up my thinking towards
other things that I included in my paper. I really saw a difference as I wrote
through the papers. Now I jot ideas down on paper and scratch it out and
write it again. It is like you first can think of something but that is not the way
it goes on the paper. I wrote it over like five times because it just didn't sound
right . . . You can't always read your own paper and say just anything because
you got in your mind that it is right.*

*When I state something I can't just state it. I have to go on. Maybe instead of
just writing something and bringing it to class I could ask my own self the
questions others might ask. Like, what does this really mean—to me—to them.*

Process and Radical Revision

What I find so valuable about this sort of assignment is the way it forces us to
consider different dimensions of our subjects (as writers and readers). Reading
the piece offers a different sort of reading experience that goes against our desire
for coherence and unity. Instead it paints an impression of Tiffany and her
response to the assignment that forces us to read the white spaces and the order
of the passages as well as the text itself. There is more work—or should I say
a different kind of work—for readers. I also feel the assignment has the poten-
tial to guide us as writers towards thoughtful insights into our own writing
processes and to help us as we look at the motives and choices we make as
writers. As a way of considering the multiple meanings for writers and readers
the core of the assignment rests in a reflective narrative on the writing and
thinking processes we go through as we radically revise. Since we have seen
that alternate style texts require different sorts of reading and evaluation strategies than traditional texts (see other articles in this collection) I find these
process statements can provide windows for readers and writers as they make
the moves to critically analyze their own texts.

My own processes in my radical revision of this piece involved many
changes and writerly considerations. In my initial draft of "Distorting the Mirror,"
I took a more traditional approach in which I spoke of Tiffany's response to the
assignment through the voice and perspective of an academic researcher. Notice the voice, stance, and approach in the following excerpts from that draft:

In this essay I explore the ways choice in style is connected to writers' perceptions, and the ways alternative forms of writing can be used as a way of

thinking. I look specifically at one student of writing's shifting perspectives as I describe her movement through and response to alternative form assignments. This narrative represents part of a semester long naturalistic study of student writers in my own small group writing class taught through the writing center at Florida State University (1993).

Style is traditionally considered in relation to written texts and the ways writers come across on the page. Students and teachers often discuss style in terms of voice, audience, and effect. Although these are important issues, I want to focus my attention in this essay on the ways shifts in style can affect student writers perceptions and their "ways of knowing." In his book, *Forms of Intellectual and Ethical Development in the College Years: A Scheme* (1970), William Perry describes the development of students' ways of viewing the world in relation to the acquisition of knowledge. Perry categorizes these ways of knowing into four developmental stages that move students towards a broader consideration of the voices that surround them.

In her early writings Tiffany held tight to her own perspectives. In conference I often questioned her ideas and challenged her perspectives like our discussion on her neutral presence in groups. At first she felt inquiries such as these were out of my domain because they were her experiences. She would often stop her ideas short and not really look at them in relation to any larger context. For her, the term "neutral" held a particular meaning and it was difficult for her to see that others might not understand it in exactly the same way. She seemed to confuse her ownership and her development of her ideas. As her teacher I was asking her to develop on the idea that she brought up but she saw it only in terms of my intimate knowledge of that idea. I think she thought of the task of meaning making resided mainly with the writer rather than within the shared reader-writer process.

Tiffany was particularly resistant to the radical revision assignment because it asked her to work against her previous assumptions about revision. Rather than changing her texts in a step by step process, this assignment asked her to see her subject in a different way and to use revision as invention. With this assignment in particular, Tiffany began to struggle with the idea that in order to understand and communicate she needed to make meaning in relation to others and that her own view of her experiences was only one possible way of seeing things. At this point her learning attitude was more multiplistic and contextualized as she incorporated and reflected on the perspectives of others.

When I workshopped the paper with other contributors in this book, most of the comments focused on my voice, style, and audience. Several readers agreed that the style I chose was more appropriate for an audience of composition teachers or researchers, and it was suggested that I try a radical revision on my own text rather than just talk about Tiffany's response. At first, like Tiffany, I was unsure about how it might work and how different revision options might alter my purpose for writing the piece. Although I was writing about radical revision, I was hesitant to take my initial essay in that direction, because it meant trying something I hadn't tried before. It was suggested that I construct a dialogue through Tiffany's point of view as she did with her mother's point of view in her own paper. I resisted this idea, because Tiffany's original words were so strong and that it didn't seem necessary to create something when actual words were so insightful and interesting. I also felt this wouldn't work, because of the time frame that was represented in the paper, which I would have to condense to a single conversation, forfeiting the complexity of her experiences.

As I read back through the initial draft, I decided to concentrate on her words only (skipping over my own interpretations) in which I saw an interesting collage or patchwork quilt of her experiences in the class. I saw patterns of resistance and movement, which seemed more alive because they were constructed through her own lively language use. I noticed the relationship and contradiction between her resistance to the class and writing ("the teacher is always right," "Just tell me what you want and I'll do it") and her push for ownership of her ideas ("These are my ideas so they can't be wrong," "I wrote my paper the way I wanted it the first time"). I liked the revised collage draft but felt unsure about how others might read it and that it would be confusing. At this point my revision focus moved towards shaping and contextualizing. I eliminated passages that were particularly acontextualized or distracting and added new, more related passages drawn from the transcripts. Then I experimented and manipulated the fonts so readers would be able to see the divisions between the different patches in the collage, which represented the different data sources from which I drew the material (conferences, group discussions, assignments, student writing).

After printing out the revised draft a couple of times, I was happy with the way the text was shaping up visually, but I was still concerned about how it was going to stand on its own. I wondered how it would be read and whether readers would understand my purposes. It might be interesting to read, but I hoped the piece would also show writers the value and processes of radical revision. With this in mind I added the opening, which I believe helps frame the piece, and the portion following, which shows my own writing and thinking processes in relation to the textual revision.

As I rewrote the draft, I was better able to see Tiffany as a complex language user as I had to let go of my initial attempts to categorize or generalize about her. As I look back on it, I realize that although I am not there as the observer in the background my presence in the text takes the form of the choices I made as a writer. Like I required of my students, I included my own process of writing the text to demonstrate the kinds of choices and processes writers must engage in order to complete this kind of assignment. I now see the writing as not only a close analysis of one student's response to an alternate style assignment but a model of the steps and processes involved in radical revision. Participating in the process myself made me question the boundaries that exist between academic, personal, and creative writing. My first draft was safe and comfortable for me as a writer while the radical revision brought with it a whole new range of writerly and readerly concerns and a sharper understanding of my purposes and audience.

I also found it fascinating to listen to the ways others responded to the text. Some people were extremely resistant to the form and said that the piece made no sense as it was lacking transitions and coherence. Others reported having to read the text through several times before coming to some sort of understanding, and one reader used the metaphor of the experience of changing swiftly through radio stations and catching snippets of talk or ideas. Some readers responded to the ways the combination of texts (my initial and revised drafts) gave a more complete, complex portrait of Tiffany from different perspectives, and it was the reading of them in conjunction that helped them make meaning. All of the readers (even the resistant ones) of the text described a productive struggle to understand and read the white spaces between the patches to make connections in order to read the piece as a whole.

I found this process to be particularly helpful for my own writing and was pleased with the ways it pushed me in unpredictable ways. I will continue to try radical revision in my writings and encourage my students to do the same. The process makes me think of the childhood experience of gazing at myself through one of those distorted mirrors you see at sideshow carnivals and the ways you have to reconsider your reflection when it is stretched or shortened. You begin to imagine the ways you are seen by others and the ways you might see yourself as a whole or in parts. Writing can be that kind of experience as we stretch our ideas, cut them up, look at them from the inside out or try to see them through the eyes of another. Revision involves seeing and seeing again and shifts in style and perspective can help us write, think, and learn.

Works Cited

Berthoff, Ann E. 1981. *The Making of Meaning: Metaphors, Models, and Maxims for Writing Teachers*. Montclair, NJ: Boynton/Cook.

Bishop, Wendy. "Risk Taking and Radical Revision—Exploring Writing Identities Through Advanced Composition and Poetry Portfolios". Manuscript in circulation.

Perry, William. 1970. *Forms of Intellectual and Ethical Development in the College Years: A Scheme*. New York, NY: Holt, Rinehart, and Winston.

10

Claiming Language
Breaking Taboos in the Writing Classroom

Nancy Reichert

Note: What follows are student and teacher journal entries I wrote during my four years as a Ph.D. student at Florida State University. During this time I also taught in the First-Year Writing Program. I decided to use the journals, because they allowed me to best express the experiences that lead to my belief that students should have the chance to break language taboos in the writing classroom. Some entries have been changed in order to acknowledge that I am no longer the only audience for this writing.

Student Journal

August 29, 1991

Damn. Another one of those required courses someone has deemed "good for me." Advanced Studies in English. A graduate course constructed to help me learn to research and publish. Useful I guess, but how boring can you get? To think I use to think reading and writing were fun! How silly of me. And look at this course work: a reading journal, a vita, a bibliography, book reviews, a paper defining a critical term, analyses of journals, and the list goes on. I hate the course already and it hasn't even started yet. Yikes. A semester from hell.

October 10, 1991

Well, I guess I am getting something out of this oh so useful, required course, but it sure is painful. I am barely keeping up with the work—I did have to quit my second job to do so—but I am doing better in my other two courses and the two courses I am teaching are going well. I keep trying to find this work meaningful, but it still feels like grunt work. At this rate I may have to take my first incomplete. The very idea pisses me off.

Teaching Journal

November 14, 1991

I have gained some insight into my reluctance to write for my Advanced Studies course by reading through some of my first-year writing student journals. In an attempt to understand how my students feel about issues of writing, I assigned a number of journal entries on writing itself. The student discussions on "academic discourse" especially have been helpful. One student wrote the following in her journal entry:

> Acedemic writing is an assignment by a teacher to analyze something. In high school acedemic writing required little imaginitive ability and a bottle of Tylenol. The assignment of acedemic writing could include anything turned in for a grade but I consider acedemic writing any writing that is done for school (AKA this journal). I've always felt pressure when I'm forced to write on a subject. It's hard to scan your mind for exactly what to write, guessing on what sounds best. For people who do not write fluidly acedemic writing assignments are very stressful.

Now I see why my students and I are reluctant to write for teachers. Writing for teachers forces us to struggle to write about issues that don't stimulate us using language we don't usually use every day. We then attempt to give the teacher what she wants so that she gives us the grade we want. None of this seems meaningful so we resist. Are there assignments that allow us to claim our work—to even enjoy our work—even when done for a grade?

Student Journal

December 18, 1991

I just finished my work for the Advanced Studies course. You guessed it— I took my first incomplete. Hey, at least I finished my work before I took off for the Christmas holidays. Considering I hated doing most of the work, it feels soooo good to have it done. I've read back over my journal expecting it to be boring, with some sort of neutral, textbooky voice, but I am surprised. My voice surfaces in the first entry: "Education did not train men for the professions they were going to enter— we would hate that today wouldn't we?" Like usual I am lambasting America's need for education to always be driven by training issues. Why did I think that my ever-so-ironic voice was missing in this journal? Why don't I relate to what I wrote?

Teaching Journal

February 14, 1992

My Horizons First-Year Writing course is not going as well as I hoped. The course is designed to help those students who are first in their family to go to college. I have always tried to create assignments that my students will enjoy, but this class resists writing even more than my other First-Year Writing classes. They seemed to do okay with the narratives we have written, but we're now talking more about academic discourse and how they can use it, and I can feel their interest—which was never great—is dropping rapidly.

I have a feeling that the large number of minority students and the four athletes are part of the problem. They seem to resist a required English course the most. I understand resisting required English courses—after my experience as a student last semester I have to understand it. However, I don't understand how to get around it as a teacher. I am really frustrated.

February 20, 1992

Last night I was reading James Baldwin's "If Black English Isn't a Language, Then Tell Me, What Is?" and I thought, "Wow, maybe some answers to why students resist required English courses, and why African American students may resist more than others." First Baldwin says that we use language to identify the speaker and to decide if he's an insider (knows standard English) or if he's an outsider (doesn't know it). Then he states:

> The brutal truth is that the bulk of the white people in America never had any interest in educating black people, except as this could serve white purposes. It is not the black child's language that is in question, it is not his language that is despised: It is his experience. A child cannot be taught by anyone who despises him, and a child cannot afford to be fooled. A child cannot be taught by anyone whose demand, essentially, is that the child repudiate his experience, and all that gives him sustenance, and enter a limbo in which he will no longer be black, and in which he knows that he can never become white. Black people have lost too many black children that way. (39)

Students, especially minority students, don't trust teachers to offer them assignments that value their experiences and language. Almost all of the students in the Horizons class have been fighting a system which they think is set up to make them fail, for it fails to value their home language. Even students like me who have done well in the system feel alienated when confronted with course work that seems meaningless, but that must be done in order to get the degree.

My minority students and my ball players also recognize that if they do fail at their schooling certain inferences will be made about their race or about their ability to succeed off the field. I must ask myself if I have been a part of a system helping students to feel as though their own lives and persons are not valued? I have to answer "yes." So, how do I better serve my students?

March 12, 1992

I think I have at least a partial answer to serving my students better. I tell my students that they cannot write what they consider to be academic discourse for their fourth papers. Instead I tell them they must write in a form that is more consistent with their home backgrounds, or that is more comfortable to them. They also must use their home language. I ask them only to provide definitions of words I may not know. They seem a little stunned. One woman asks a little defiantly, "Can I write a rap?" She thinks that I don't really mean what I say—she knows raps are not privileged discourse in the university. I answer, "Yes, whatever brings your home environment to me will work."

March 25, 1992

I have looked over my students' fourth papers, and I have found the papers show an investment missing in the previous work. The one woman did write a rap—about raps. Her investment is clear as she questions the violence and the sexism that she finds often in rap music. In the end, she does claim the music as a part of her community, for it voices the rage, love, and experience of her people. Another student's play attempts to demonstrate the unending circle of violence that he sees encompassing some of his best friends. One act of violence calls for another act of violence. The language is violent, descriptive, and often foreign to me. He provides a glossary of terms for me defining even words I do know such as "crib" and "hood."

Only a student or two have worried that such an assignment is not appropriate for a classroom. They worry about the assignment's utility. I tell them that it has done for me exactly what I wished it to do: allowed students to care about what they wrote—allowed them to work hard so that they could say it just right. I have deemed the paper a success and I have already asked students to radically revise an earlier paper in a similar manner.

Student Journal

December 12, 1992

I have been thinking about this past year a bit. I am amazed at the risks I have begun to take in my writing. Since I have begun pushing students to write from their own lives and to break with tradition, I have begun to push my own writing in similar ways. This past fall I thought the seminar I took on American literary cultures would be a repeat of my Advanced Studies course. In fact, I began the semester cussing over the assignments just as I had done before. However, I took risks and even made an assignment defining literary terms my own. I created definitions-in-progress in order to push my idea that the meaning of words continue to evolve. For example, I defined "culture" in the following way:

> Actually this is quite a vague term. People use it all the time and mean different things by it. However, people do seem to use the term to define themselves and their time period—to try and reach an understanding of the boundaries of acceptable practice, and some-

times to stretch those boundaries and to redefine them. Those peoplle
working within the set cultural boundaries are rewarded with prizes
or at least nods of respect. Those trying to stretch the boundaries
may be ignored or may be punished through exile, imprisonment,
and so on. (Greenblatt, 226)

My risks paid off and I found myself enjoying writing tasks I usually
considered "grunt" work. I learned more, and I finished the course without
needing an incomplete. I managed to write for myself and the course at the
same time. Most of the anxiety, resistance, and self-questioning I experienced
with the Advanced Studies rarely surfaced once I decided to take over the
assignments. Maybe I'll make it through graduate school after all.

February 20, 1993

Yes! I have found another important passage for teaching the paper concerned
with breaking boundaries! I was reading for a class I am taking concerned
with the history of rhetoric when I read this passage from Michel Foucault's
The Order of Discourse:

In a society like ours, the procedures of exclusion are well known.
The most obvious and familiar is the prohibition. We know quite
well that we do not have the right to say everything, that we cannot speak of just anything in any circumstances whatever, and that
not everyone has the right to speak of anything whatever. (1155)

As soon as I read this, it reminded me of Baldwin because it too speaks
of the power of language. However, what Foucault says is that we don't
always have the right to say what we want to say and that certain circumstances and certain people help to dictate what we can and can't say. Foucault
also states that these language taboos "intersect, reinforce, and compensate
for each other, forming a complex grid which changes constantly. . . .
the regions where the grid is tightest, . . . are those of sexuality and politics"
(1155). That seems exactly right. Some circumstances and some people make
it more difficult to talk about already taboo topics such as sex. For example,
as a student in a classroom, I would never tell the teacher, "Sorry, I didn't hear
your question because I was thinking about the great sex I had with my boyfriend last night."

Let's face it, taboos traditionally tell students they cannot speak to teachers in classrooms let alone tell those teachers that they got laid. Don't students
normally sit quietly taking down the "important" words of the professor? It
seems to me that the more distant the language of the home is from the privileged language of the university the more the student will feel powerless to
speak in a classroom where the teacher has the authority and the classroom
is not a comfortable site. I can remember sitting in classrooms trying to frame
a question in my mind just right, finally asking the teacher it, and stuttering
because I was so worried about saying it well.

Hell, no wonder some of the Horizon students have more problems than
the students who are raised using Standard English with writing and speaking
for teachers. No wonder almost all of my students feel as though they are
outsiders trying to figure out the rules to become insiders.

Teaching Journal

March 2, 1993

Foucault has supplied me with more than an excerpt for the paper I teach challenging writing boundaries. He has also supplied me with a name and an invention technique. I will call the paper "The Taboo-Breaking Paper," and I will have students create three grids. These grids will concern topics which we feel we cannot speak on freely. The grids will help to establish what people silence us, what circumstances silence us, and what types of writing may silence us. The grids should help my classes to understand what taboos are a part of our culture and a part of writing in the university, and they should help my students to understand how to go about breaking with established writing rules concerning what kind of writing is acceptable for a composition classroom as well as what kind of writing frees them to write about what are normally taboo subjects.

March 6, 1993

Today I had students read the excerpt from Foucault concerning language taboos. I then had them break into pairs and work on summarizing the excerpt. Once we had talked about the excerpt, we began to create the grids. We began with the vertical side of the first grid with the words "sexuality" and "politics" since Foucault has already addressed these two topics as taboo. I then asked students to name other taboo topics and they named topics such as "religion," "homosexuality," "race," "bodily functions" and so on. The vertical line of the grid was complete. I then asked students what types of people they encounter, and gave the example of teacher. They named people such as "police officer," "parent," "same sex friend," "opposite sex friend," "different race friend" and so on. I wrote these types of people horizontally at the bottom of the grid so that a short version of such a grid looks something like this:

sex			
politics			
religion			
	teacher	police officer	parent

People you may encounter

I asked students to copy the grid onto a sheet of paper and asked them to begin shading the grid. I told them if they can speak freely of the topic to the person to leave the square blank. I told them to shade in from lightest to darkest as they feel more powerless to speak freely about the topic to the person. We then did two more grids changing horizontal lines so that we also look at circumstance (classroom, home, church and so on) and types of writing (formal essay, journal, freewriting and so on). Students better understood the writing assignment which was to write about a topic they normally found to be taboo using a style, a grammar, or a genre which would help them write about the topic, but which was normally taboo to use in a writing classroom.

Here are my grids from the classroom. The more the squares are filled in with x's the more likely I would **not** feel comfortable speaking my personal views on a certain issue to a certain person, in a certain situation, or in a certain type of writing. I learned that I never feel completely free to say what I want: there are no completely blank spaces. My students exclaimed over this. They had thought that I had spoken freely with them. I hope they begin to question what it really means to speak freely.

Grid One

politics	xxxx	xx	xxxxx	xxxxxxxx	x
sexuality	xxxxxxx	x	xx	xxxxxxxx	xxxxxxxxxx
religion	xxxxxxxx	xxx	xxxxx	xxxxxxxxx	xxx
bodily functions	xxxxxxxxx	xxx	xxxxxxxx	xxxxxxx	xxxxxxx
racism	xxxxxxxx	xxx	xxxxx	xxxxxxxxxx	xxx
cussing*	xxxxxxxx	xx	xxx	xxxxxxxxxx	xxxxxx
	teacher	friend/ same race or same gender	friend/ dif. race- or dif. gender	police office	parent

People you may talk to during your day.

Grid Two

politics	xxxxx	x	xxxxxx	xxxxxxxxxx	xxx
sexuality	xxxxxxxxx	x	xxxxxxxx	xxxxxxxxxx	xx
religion	xxxxxxx	xx	xxxx	xxxx	xxxxxxx
bodily functions	xxxxxxxxxx	xxx	xxxxxxxxxx	xxxxxxxxxx	xxxxxx
racism	xxxxxxx	xx	xxxxxxxxxx	xxxxxxxxxx	xxxxx
cussing*	xxxxxx	x	xxxxxxxxx	xxxxxxxxxx	xxx
	classroom	in your home	on a first date	in church	at a party

Circumstances you may find yourself in during your day.

Grid Three

politics	xxxx	xx	xx	xxxxx	xxx
sexuality	xxxxxxxxxx	x	xxx	xxxxxxxxxx	xxxxx
religion	xxxxxxx	x	xxx	xxxxxxxx	xxxx

	research paper	diary or journal	freewrite	expository paper	short story or narrative
bodily functions	XXXXXXXXXX	XXXX	XXXXXXXXXX	XXXXXXXXXX	XXXXXXXXXX
racism	XXXXXXX	XX	XXXX	XXXXXXX	XXXX
cussing*	XXXXXXXXXX	X	X	XXXXXXXXX	XXX

Types of writing you may use

(Keep in mind: the more x's, the more discomfort with the topic when talking to a certain type of person, in a certain circumstance, and with the type of writing.)

* Cussing concerns using the words our culture has deemed profane, not discussing using these types of words.

June 15, 1995

I have taught the taboo-breaking paper for the last time at Florida State University, for I am graduating and have a job elsewhere. One of the more risky student papers this six weeks was "In the Name of the Father, and of the Son and of the Holy Spirit" by Amy Wiegand. According to Amy she wrote the paper because she feels out of touch with the Catholic Church. She writes, "This generation's norms totally contradict what religion professes, such as premarital sex, birth control, abortion, and homosexuality." To show the difference she wanted to put the reader in her head during a mass. Here's one section from her paper:

> We believe in God
> the father, the almighty,

Well, Mr. Almighty better hook me up tonight, I hope that stuff isn't bad,

> maker of heaven and earth,
> of all that is seen and unseen.

Some things should be unseen like that Girl's dress in front of me, Give me some sunglasses!

> We believe in one Lord, Jesus Christ,

yeah, I might believe in this God, but I can't believe he would make an asshole like Todd.

> the only Son of God,
> eternally begotten of the Father,
> God from God, Light from Light,

Did I forget to call Thagard for my pills? Shit, I better go tomorrow.

> true God from true God,
> begotten, not made, one in Being with the Father.

Better be one in Being with you know who tonight! I didn't buy my new outfit for nothing!

Reading it, I enjoy both Amy's creativity and how well I understand her point. As a fellow Catholic, I find that her paper shocks me with its irreverence, but her very irreverence is the point. How many Catholics do go to mass and reflect on other life issues? And how often do Catholics admit that their church may not respond to the issues of the times? Although the paper started out difficult for her, she ended up expressing satisfaction with what she accomplished. I too think Amy has accomplished her goal, and I enjoyed the investment shown throughout her drafts.

Student Journal

June 3, 1995

I have recently finished my Ph.D. program. Of course, I don't feel finished. I do know that my increased ability to find ways to make assigned writing my own helped me to write my dissertation. More importantly it helped me to enjoy writing it. Revealing the taboos for conscious discussion has helped my students and me to understand what it means to write for a grade. It has helped me to understand the parameters of writing assignments so that even as I write for them I find ways to lay claim to what I say and how I say it. Conscious knowledge of the taboos has opened up an understanding of what it means to explode the traditional boundaries of writing for the academy.

Works Cited

Baldwin, James. 1987. "If Black English Isn't a Language, Then Tell Me, What Is?" *Modern American Prose*. 2nd ed. Ed. John Clifford and Robert DiYanni. New York, NY: McGraw. 37–40.

Foucault, Michel. 1990. *The Order of Discourse. The Rhetorical Tradition*. Ed. Patricia Bizzell and Bruce Herzberg. Boston, MA: St. Martin's Press. 1154–1164.

Greenblatt, Stephen. 1990. "Culture." *Critical Terms for Literary Study*. Ed. Frank Lentricchia and Thomas McLaughlin. Chicago, IL: U of Chicago Press. 225–232.

11

"You Want Us to Do WHAT?"
How to Get the Most Out of Unexpected Writing Assignments

Ruth Mirtz

The students were stunned. They looked at their teacher. They looked at each other. They knew how to react to a pop quiz, but this was different. Finally, one student found her voice, raised her hand, and asked, "You want us to do WHAT?"

Miss Rachel explained the assignment again. "So, your next paper is actually a revision of your last paper, the one I just handed back. Except this paper will be purely experimental. Break one or two of the rules of good writing and see what happens."

"You want us to write bad?" asked the same brave student.

"Badly. No, I'm thinking of the traditional rules of good school writing. Like 'a paragraph must logically follow the previous paragraph.'"

Miss Rachel picked up the chalk and started writing on the board.

"You mean, like, use transitions?" asked a student.

"Right. What else?" asked Miss Rachel writing on the chalkboard:

- Use transitions.
- Must have complete sentences.
- Paragraphs must have at least 3 sentences.
- No surface errors—follow grammar rules.
- Be clear.
- Be concise—don't go on a tangent.

"Okay, that's not a complete list. We could think of all sorts of other rules to break. I know this sounds weird and impossible, but I want you to write something you've never even thought of writing before, and I think this assignment will force you to do just that," Miss Rachel said. "It's time to go now, but start thinking about it now and we'll talk more about it at the next class period."

Cody shuffled out, grumbling. "She's crazy, man. There's no way I'm doing it."

Wanda shook her head as she collected her book bag, water bottle, jacket, and umbrella. "I hope she tells us more on Wednesday. I don't get it at all."

Shiv smiled. "I'm glad we're finally getting to do a creative assignment. I always do better on papers when I can do it the way I want."

Tamika went straight to Miss Rachel after class was dismissed and asked her about the assignment. "How long does it have to be? Are you going to grade us on this? Could I just write a book report? I have three exams next week and I have to start everything early," she explained.

The next day, Miss Rachel handed out an assignment sheet:

ENC1101-45 Nov. 12, 1994

Grammar B

Grammar is essentially a set of conventions that everyone agrees to follow. Grammar A is the set of conventions that produces formal, standard English, the set you've been learning and required to reproduce in all your papers for school. Grammar B is another set of rules that only certain professional writers get away with, but which produces meaning much more accurately and expressively for certain occasions. Winston Weathers' article "Grammars of Style" (in *Rhetoric and Composition*, Ed. R. Graves, 1984. Portsmouth, NH: Boynton/Cook Heinemann, 1984) is my source for this handout.

Below are some ways you can use Grammar B in the next version.

1. **Crots.** A crot is a "chunk" of sentences or text that all goes together in some way. It looks like a "note" without the text that it's notating. You could write a series of crots as "snapshots" separated by space or asterisks.

2. **Labyrinthine Sentences.** A long, winding, endless sentence which usually follows Grammar A within phrases but not necessarily in the sentences as a whole, which may use parentheses, series set off by semicolons, embedded phrases, explanations within explanations (such as why this particular sentence is not really a very labyrinthine sentence because it is too short and too straightforward).

3. **Sentences Fragments.** Use them. Often. To give a sense of uncertainty. Or separation.

4. **Lists.**   Generally   A minimum of five
                     Usually   Independent of a sentence
                     Possibly   Written horizontally or vertically or otherwise
                     Sometimes   Looks like a poem

5. **Double-voice.** Two or more competing or complementing perspectives can be written in the same text "breath" using parentheses, italics, spac-

ing, questions, or just much different styles. Yeah, right, I'm sure they understand double-voice with that incredibly hopeless sentence. Double-voicing is a dialogue without Grammar A dialogue punctuation and without the framing devices for dialogue. Geez, maybe I should write this in columns as a better example and don't I need to warn them not to overuse the computer-font/styles? Changing fonts or print styles is not double-voicing, though, so don't use computer tricks instead of thinking out your meaning. No, this belongs below with the guidelines.

6. **Synchronicity.** If the writer scrambles verb tenses and time markers, the reader got the sense that the point will be less about had a point that about becoming a point.

7. **Collage/Montage.** Crots, lists, fragments, and labyrinthine sentences, poems, descriptions, maxims, schedules, stories can be combined into a collage, a loosely organized group of different kinds of text.

Guidelines for Producing a Grammar B draft:

z. Don't change topics/it's too late now.

y. If you conceive of a Grammar B–like device that fits what you want to say (that is, breaks one rule of Grammar A to good effect).

Do it

x. Don't change font styles every other word or add obscure symbols and call it Grammar B. It won't B.

w. Have fun. Play. Take a Chance. If it Fails because you tried something that didn't work, it didn't Fail. If it fails because you didn't try, it failed.

q. Do as the handout describes, not as it does. This handout uses too many different Grammar B techniques because it's trying to illustrate possibilities rather than make sense.

v. The POINT of this assignment, which I place at the end of the handout instead of the Grammar A position at the beginning of the handout, is to understand better what Grammar A is all about by using Grammar B, to explore what Grammar A (and Grammar B, perhaps) fails to express, to be politically aware (instead of politically correct) of who gets to make rules like Grammar A and who doesn't, who gets to use Grammar B and why, what the rules of Grammar A accomplish in terms of communication, expression, meaning-making, to explore further the concept of revision by writing a radically different version of a paper and comparing the effect, and to imagine more possibilities and power in language than Grammar A (or our assumptions and ignorances about Grammar A) allows us.

The next week, when the first drafts were due, Tamika brought a poem about her small hometown and its lack of excitement. Her friends thought it sounded great, were jealous that Tamika's paper was already done, and had a hard time telling her what she was trying to say in the paper. "I just broke the lines up from my last draft into shorter lines. It looks like a poem now. It's just a first draft," she said.

Cody didn't bring a draft. "I still don't get it," he said. He rolled his eyes when Miss Rachel replied, "Then we'd better talk after class."

Wanda brought a sheaf of handwritten pages: two pages of lists, a page of paragraphs, and her last draft cut into pieces. "I know it was supposed to be typed, and I was supposed to bring copies, but I'm sure I didn't do it right. I'll ask Miss Rachel if I did it right, and then I'll bring copies next week? I don't get what a crot is," she asked her peer response group.

"I thought they were clots," said one group member.

"No, it's *crots*, whatever that is," insisted Wanda, "and, anyway, I don't get it."

Shiv brought a draft written in two columns. "I think this is double-voice. At least, that's what I was trying for."

"Do we read it across or down each column?" asked a group member.

"I don't know. I didn't think of reading it across the columns. Let's try it both ways and see which way you like better," Shiv proposed.

After discussing the first drafts in class, Miss Rachel asked them what they were thinking. "I know you've been confused by this unexpected assignment, and I think we should talk about how you've been dealing with the assignment. What have you been telling yourself as you've been working on this paper?" The class came up with a rough list of statements on the chalkboard, argued about which ones were "excuses" and which ones were "strategies," and talked about other assignments that had been difficult, different, or unexplainable. Everyone had a story about the strangest assignment a teacher had ever given them: chanting before writing, turning a research paper into a poem, writing for space aliens, writing without seeing the computer screen, and so on. Miss Rachel typed up the list for the next class period and added her own explanations of the items:

ENC1101-45 November 14, 1994

Ways We Handle Unexpected Writing Assignments

Writers deal with unexpected assignments by finding ways to make the assignment safe for them. Some of the strategies we've used are these

1. "I'd call this assignment one of those "impossible" or "wacko" assignments. Once I put it in that category, I can treat it with contempt and do as little as possible." *We might call this attitude "objectification": deciding this assignment belongs in a certain "wacko" or "beyond me" category. The quicker we can label a writing assignment, the better we feel about it.*

2. "I'm sure there's some benefit to this assignment for someone besides me, but this has nothing to do with me." *We might call this projection: putting the benefits of the assignment on someone else's shoulders.*

3. "If my teacher would just tell me what she wants in this assignment, then we could just move on." *We could call this "getting practical" but we could also call it a strategy of "pragmatism." When I hear myself putting*

all the emphasis on the word "just," I know I'm looking for a quick way out.

4. "I could do this assignment, if she would just explain it better." *My mother used to tell me this is called "shifting the blame" and I was very good at it when I was a student.*

5. "I'll just do the least I can on this assignment and make it up by doing better on other assignments." *Maybe this strategy is "surrendering the will to an A." Calculating my grade and the amount of time I wanted to spend on other activities got me to this strategy in record time.*

6. "I'm just too dumb to figure this out." *Self-blame is always good for some sympathy from friends.*

7. "The teacher hates me and is trying to get me." *This excuse shifts the responsibility or blame, too.*

8. "I didn't pay hundreds of dollars of tuition to learn this stuff. This school should teach me only what I want to learn." *Blaming the whole educational system is a good way to let everyone off the hook for the assignment.*

Tamika complained, "This makes us sound like a bunch of lazy people looking for excuses."

"Yeah, but I use these excuses for all my assignments," Cody said, "not just the ones that I don't want to do."

"Hey, we probably use these for all sorts of things, like relationships," Wanda suggested.

"Maybe we should all go on the Rikki Lake Show," suggested another student.

"Well, if these ways of reacting to strange assignments were the first and last thing we did, we would be good candidates for Rikki and Geraldo. But we generally manage to get the worst assignments completed, right? We move past these excuses and rationalizations," Miss Rachel reminded them, in her "this-isn't-high-school-anymore" voice.

At the next class, Miss Rachel handed them a list of "safer" strategies for dealing with the assignment:

ENC1101-45 November 21, 1994

Ways Writers Get Past Their Excuses

All these strategies work to a degree, but the problem is when we stop with one of these strategies and stop thinking about the assignment any more. Here's some ways I think you might transform some safe positions to risky positions:

1. Okay, so it's "dumb" or "wacko." What ELSE is it?

2. Okay, so this assignment has nothing to do with you. What might it have to do with the person you might want to be someday?

3. Okay, so the teacher refuses to tell you what she wants. What do YOU want to do?

4. Okay, so it's your teacher's fault. What questions could you ask her about the assignment that would help you understand it better?

5. Okay, so you won't get an A on this assignment. What will keep you from getting a C on this assignment?

6. Okay, so you aren't a great writer. How do poor writers become good writers?

7. Okay, so your teacher hates you specifically. How might you win her over by doing this assignment?

8. Okay, so you're losing money doing this dumb stuff. Which jobs come with complete instructions for every writing task. (There actually are a few—find out what they are and see if you are interested in those jobs.)

Shiv and Wanda both arranged for a conference with Miss Rachel before the final versions were due. Shiv brought his final draft and wanted Miss Rachel to read it and tell him if she thought it met the assignment's guidelines. Miss Rachel actually made him read it aloud to her in her office and explain to her why HE thought it fit the assignment. When he had given her all the reasons he could think of, she said she was convinced. Shiv left her office, shaking his head. "I wish she would just tell me what to do, instead of asking me to defend what I've already done," he thought to himself.

Wanda was a mess. She still had several handwritten rough drafts and she had a big history test the same day this assignment was due. "Can't I just write another paper, like the last one we did?" she asked Miss Rachel in her office. "Or, do you, like, give extra credit assignments if I don't do this one?"

"You've already got a good start on this assignment. Your small group liked your ideas, right?" asked Miss Rachel. "Tell me about what you have so far."

Wanda explained what she had in mind with her crots, why she couldn't get it on paper, and why she couldn't possibly have it done by the next day. Miss Rachel was adamant, though: no extra credit, do the best possible by to-morrow, and if Wanda needed to revise afterward, they would talk. Miss Rachel reminded her that the point of the assignment was to try something she had never written before, to explore some other ways of writing. "You're right that your crots aren't like the ones we talked about in class. These crots read just like the paragraphs in your last essay. Grammar A is very linear, and one idea describes how it's connected to the next one. But crots use emphasis and rep-etition to make those connections, not transitions."

"But I can't write that way. This is the only way I know how to write."

"But! But you sort of write in crots in your very early drafts. I've read them. You jump from one thing to another, some paragraphs aren't finished, you aren't sure what order they should be in. Now you can go back to those chunks of writing, but finish each one as a mini-essay, or like chapters in a books, or like prequels and sequels to the original movie."

"Oh," said Wanda. "I guess I can do that. How long are the crots supposed to be?"

"You decide. How long do they *need* to be?" said Ms. Rachel.

"Geez, this is the hardest paper we've done yet," Wanda said.

"Do you think so? I think it's the one you've resisted the most."

"I suppose so. I'm making this harder than it really is, aren't I?"

"Maybe. I'll be eager to see what you come up with, in any case."

On the day the final draft was due, Miss Rachel first asked them to give their papers a final editing before handing them in. Then she asked them to write a memo to her about the assignment, describing how they wrote the assignment and what they thought they learned from it. While they were writing, Cody came in and whispered to Miss Rachel that he didn't have his paper.

"You know I don't accept late papers," Miss Rachel said. "I know," Cody replied. "Let's talk after class," Miss Rachel said. Cody found a chair and sat, while the rest of the class wrote the memo.

Memo for Grammar B paper—Nov. 26—Wanda J.

I read through the worksheet and tried to understand Grammar B. When writing my paper I attempted to incorporate this unconventional method. I thought "I can't do this." I did try, though, to condense my points and write bits of ideas for my crots. I'm still not sure if it's the best way to do it.

Miss Rachel asked Tamika, Shiv, and three other students to read their final versions to the class (see Appendix for one example). Cody left after class without talking to Miss Rachel.

At the next class, Miss Rachel was supposed to give them the next paper assignment. "But I want to talk more about the last assignment first," she said, handing out this sheet.

ENC1101-45 November 28, 1994

Responses to the Last Assignment

Things that we discovered by doing an unexpected assignment, by writing in a new style, by being forced out of a comfortable position:

1. I realized that I use the rules of "normal" writing just to add a lot of "fluff" and "bull."

2. I had to get to the point, finally.

3. Being indirect is sometimes more powerful.

4. Now I see what "normal" writing really is; now I see what the rules are. I realize I usually have to think in normal structure in order to write in normal structure. One thing that I noticed was how my mind has been engraved with Grammar A, which seems to leave no room for other techniques.

5. What I thought was stupidity, bad writing, or bad thinking was really a different style of writing and thinking. Now I see that I can write a rough draft in my made-up style and then switch to get a formal version.

6. "Normal" writing sometimes won't let me say what I really want to say.

7. I really hate change. I like Grammar A lot better. I have worked hard to learn it for the last 12 years and all of a sudden you want me to write run-ons and sentence fragments! I think my high school teachers would fall down in their tracks!

8. I thought it would be easier to write in an unusual style, but it was harder.

"I don't think you would have confronted some of these issues, if you hadn't done this assignment," said Miss Rachel.

"But we can't write in Grammar B in our other classes, can we?" said Tamika.

"We can do our rough drafts in lists and winding sentences, if it helps us figure out what to say," countered Wanda.

"And some of it, like the lists, is more like what I write at work," said Shiv. "You know, manuals often have lists instead of paragraphs. And you have to get right to the point."

"So, what shall I tell my students next semester when I give this assignment?" asked Miss Rachel.

"Be sick that week," piped up Wanda, and everyone laughed and clapped.

One of Cody's friends leaned over to Wanda and whispered, "I guess that's what Cody did. He isn't here today, and he hasn't done any of the drafts."

Wanda whispered back, "I saw him at the union this morning." The two shrugged their shoulders and turned back to the front of the classroom.

"Okay, okay," Miss Rachel said, after the talk died down. "What would actually be helpful?"

A long pause gave everyone time to think. Miss Rachel walked to the chalkboard and picked up the chalk, so they knew she wanted them to contribute.

"Don't procrastinate," said Wanda. "These revisions took longer than any of the others, because I had never written something like this before, and it took me a long time to figure out what you wanted."

"Good," said Miss Rachel, writing on the board. "What else?"

"Have a conference," added Wanda. "I didn't get it until I talked to you in your office."

"Sure. Some people find it easier to ask questions privately, right?" said Miss Rachel. "Who else has some advice for my students next semester?"

Eventually, the class came up with this list on the board.

- Don't procrastinate—experiments take more time.
- Have a conference—ask about grades!—ask more questions.
- Get used to being confused.
- Keep all your attempts—first might/might not be best.
- Write someplace different—use different materials (crayons, etc.).
- Don't plagiarize (could get kicked out of school).
- Don't waste time arguing—do it like any other assignment.

After making the list, Miss Rachel said they had given her some good ideas for when she makes the assignment again. Then Tamika asked loudly, "Did you know we've talked more about DOING this assignment than we've talked about what we actually WROTE?"

Miss Rachel laughed and said, "Now you're getting the point! And if you thought that last assignment was crazy, listen to the next one . . ."

APPENDIX

J. Ryan Roberts

I carefully placed the pillow under the sheets. I pondered to myself and decided not to go and ask my parents if I could go to my friend's house. I figured they would never know and plus what if they say "no." So I locked my bedroom door and snuck out my window like a thief. The air was cold and I had energy flowing through my body. I was free. I could do anything I wanted until my parents awoke from their slumber state.

"What time is it?" I said as I awoke to the sun's light. "Nine o'clock in the morning." I knew that my chances of getting away with sneaking out were definitely slim. I walked home only to find that my window (my means of escape from my parent's house) was now locked. Since I had not locked it, I knew I had been caught. My stomach dropped and all the energy I had the night before had left my body. I could not believe that I had fallen asleep. I was very mad at myself.

Opposites attract, or so they say. I guess that is why my parents have been married for twenty-three years. My mother was raised by a very old fashioned and strict father. My dad was brought up in a small southern town with religious parents. The nature of my father is to be different and to be in control. He is a self-made man who started from scratch. Considering my mother has been by his side for twenty-three years, maybe I should say a self-made man with a little help. They have had two children. I happen to be the oldest. Being the oldest represents the first attempt at parenthood. Being a parent is not easy, it is a lifelong responsibility that requires a lot of time, money, and effort. Until a couple of months ago, I did not realize how much work being a parent is.

I have never understood why my parents were more strict with me than they are with my brother. I guess since I was their first child they wanted to make sure they stressed discipline and just wanted to be good parents. I was allowed one soda a day and minimal junkfood intake. I was never allowed to get cereal with sugar in it, so I grew up on Cheerios and Rice Krispies. My brother on other hand has not had to worry about those petty rules. With my brother's birth, my parents grew less strict. I have never been able to explain why, but I have observed the obvious change.

My parents and I have a special relationship that I feel all parents and kids should have. I can be very open with them. They know everything I have done and tried. They know my morals and my values, and not only do they know them, but they respect them. Ever since I was caught sneaking out, my parents and I have been more open with each other. We have had our rough times, but they are generally few and short. I wish everyone could talk to their parents as openly and honestly as I can. My parents are my friends as well as my disciplinarians, and they are able to keep a perfect balance with each aspect of our relationship.

My parents are very understanding people. When I was in the sixth grade I drove our Jeep Cherokee through the wall that divides the garage from our dining room. To my surprise, my parents did not kill me. My mother was not quite as understanding as my father, but he got her to settle down. I was young and not very familiar with how to drive a car. I put the car in drive on accident and rather than going backward, I started creeping toward the wall of the garage. I then panicked and got confused about which pedal was the gas and which was the brake. I ended up pushing the wrong pedal and drove the Cherokee through the wall.

Not only has college been a growing period for me as an individual, but it has also been a growing period for my relationship with my parents. Since I have been away at college, my parents and I have taken each other for granted less. I think living with people causes you to take them more for granted. Now that I do not live with them, they trust that they have raised me well and trust my judgment. I know that any time I am having a bad day, I can call my parents and they will help me out. I just feel better after talking to them. I realize how fortunate I am to have such understanding friends in my parents.

Memo about my writing process:

1. I wrote this draft by writing thought or segments of thought that I had last night. Basically I thought about my relationship with my parents and wrote about important events, both good and bad, that have occurred over the years.

2. I was trying to show why I feel I have a good relationship with my mom and dad. I felt that showing some good times and some bad times would help give a well-rounded view about our relationship. I wanted to give bad times as examples as well as good times so my paper would not sound like a fairy tale.

3. I chose to use the snapshot technique because I feel it is the most effective. I think small detailed "thought photos" is an interesting methods of getting thoughts across.

4. If I had more time, I think I would incorporate lists in my paper. I think

lists get the most across with the least amount of words. It would have been an interesting experiment.

5. As I worked on this paper, I was reminded how restrictive Grammar A is and how much more freedom I had with Grammar B. I would use Grammar B in other classes for brainstorming, because I can write my thoughts without worrying about the rules of Grammar A.

III

Issues in Writing in Alternate Styles

12

Reading, Stealing, and Writing Like a Writer

Wendy Bishop

Recently, I was hired by a local lawyer to be an expert witness on the sentence for an upcoming court case. What he asked me to do, as a writer and teacher of writers, was to give him a "standard" or "customary" reading of a legal statute. Thinking about this, I realized, that when I write poems, I do have to be an expert on words. And I can be an expert witness on the sentence because I'm constantly analyzing the sentences I read to compose the sentences I want to write.

I don't just read and write sentences (nor am I particularly good at analyzing them using conventional grammar), but I find sentences to be sculptural, like clay, sometimes, things that writers bend, shape, and mold to their purposes. I think of sentences as alive, responding here when pushed there, resisting here and obliging there. I've come to understand prose—first on the meaning level of what is being said—but also on the literal, syntactical level, as if touching and counting a string of beads, with all my attention tuned high. Then, I steal like a writer to write like a writer, using sentences to make my variation on the common themes and genres that all writers share—love story to technical report.

It wasn't always this way, this love affair with sentences. When I was an undergraduate in college, like many of my students I felt like I just *read*. It wasn't until I claimed the sentence as my area of desire, interest, and expertise—until I wanted to be a writer writing better—that I had to look underneath my initial readings. Soon, I had to question my emotional or story response to a text. It was no longer enough to report my response—hot, cold, or indifferent—or to ask what happened next as the paragraphs went down the page. I started asking, *how*—*how* did the writer get me to feel, *how* did the writer say something so that it remains in my memory when many other things too easily fall out, *how* did that writer communicate his/her intentions about genre, about irony?

A few years ago, I read the ideas of reading theorist Louise Rosenblatt who pointed out that we can look at the same texts in different ways and in doing so, read them differently: The texts don't change, our reasons for and attitudes towards reading change. (She also claims that each of our readings—even of the same text—are different because we are different, but that's another discussion). We can read instrumentally—to extract information. We usually do this when reading telephone books, textbooks, and reports. Or efferently, to experience the effects of the text, often aesthetic effects: the pain of a love story, the passion of a fine political speech, the life-transforming power of a religious text.

I'm thinking nowadays that it's good to learn to do both, at will—that is, sometimes you can get around a difficult textbook by trying to enjoy it— analyze the style of the writer, try to figure out how she or he even managed to write that way—and for fun you can read the phone book like a poem by looking at the alliteration of the names and streets—Wanda Wallace lives on Woodbine Way. What I want to do as a reading, stealing, writing writer is both, learning to inhabit, often, the middle ground. I need to cultivate double vision. I need both to feel the effects and also to extract the information about how those effects are achieved. I can enjoy the nursery rhyme rhythm of Wanda Wallace on Woodbine Way, but I can't write it myself—unless I analyze (look at all those Ws, listen to the rhythm) and imitate (steal?!) and put together my own pleasurable prose: Randal Reader lives on Writer Road. Look what I've done here—changed gender, made a play on the subject of my paragraph and the subject of writing. Cheap thrills, but that's how a writer reads to write.

You may not think of yourself as reader and writer. But you are doing both in the broadest sense all the time. You're reading your world every day; you compose your life. In the kitchen each A.M., you read the cupboards and refrigerator for breakfast options, cereal to eggs to bagels. You read the weather and read your closet, choosing your clothes by a complicated writer's formula: what's clean, what represents who I want to be today, what's appropriate for the weather? You read the newspaper, perhaps, choosing quickly which story engages you and which you don't need to read further. You read everyone at work or school. You read the signs and ads and marquees on your way home and write your evening plan in your head: go to the mall, stop in to listen to the band at X, or stay home and watch Y on TV. You steal your daily habits from your family (think about Thanksgiving meals), your friends (there are clothes you borrow, sayings you pick up), your developing age and tastes (as a child you never ate artichokes, but now . . .) You steal the right office or school moves by watching others in the same or similar situations. You see what I mean, I think.

So let's go back to this thing I'll define as reading like a writer—I could call it developing rhetorical fluency—but I won't. Let me show you how sentences are all around you waiting to be understood, stolen, modified, used by you in your writing. What I'm talking about are not the sentences given to you in school writing rules. You already know those, and you've practiced them or not as you've chosen. I can think of a fast few here. Don't start a sentence with coordinating conjunctions *and*, *so*, *but*, etc. Don't write single sentence paragraphs. All sentences have a subject and predicate (verb). Generally, don't use first person (I), slang, or profanity. Use exclamation points sparingly! Be clear, concise, and coherent. Argue logically. Etc. Now you may not have heard all these rules or heard them phrased just this way, but I bet you have a lot of writing etiquette packed in your brain somewhere. Try it—just for a minute free-write the rules that come to mind, like I just did.

Included in this list—embedded in this list—is the idea that good writers write right and people who break the rules should know better (don't know better) and should be corrected. Correct? But that's a matter of making our language inflexible, and remember how I mentioned the way—as a writer—I've come to feel sentences are alive, fluid and flexible, wild and tamed at times but not any one thing, always. Did you notice that sentence began with a co-ordinating conjunction? I didn't until I was done drafting since I was most interested in pursuing this idea, sharing it with you.

My argument: if you start to study sentences as a writer does, you'll see that they're more varied and flexible, a better instrument for exploring and expressing thought, than maybe you ever knew. The rules we're "given" can only address a small part of our language repertoire and are most often constraining and constricting rather than elucidating and explaining. It makes sense to follow the rules to get to where you want to go—especially during initial drafting, *for if you don't know what you're saying, your reader surely won't*. But later, as you revise, the possibilities of language should make you want to play, to match meaning to your own sentence magic, to create what we call style—your own best way of saying.

Here's another analogy. It makes sense that when we sit down together at dinner, we're more comfortable if everyone eats in a fairly civilized way— spoons, forks, food moving from plate to mouth in a compact and regular manner. I don't want spaghetti splashed all over the wood floor and staining the carpet, and it would make me queasy to eat off someone else's greasy plate. Fine. But there are occasions when such an orchestrated eating arrangement may be less than useful (or pleasurable): Don't sit me on the back patio eating a wonderful summer watermelon with a tiny silver spoon and napkin. Let me take a chunk in my fingers and bite into the red meat with my teeth and enjoy the sweet drip down my chin. I'll wash at the hose in a minute.

The same with sentences. If all our sentences, all our prose, followed "the rules" and showed good taste and fine manners . . . we'd lose something. We'd be bored to death. We wouldn't "hear" much from texts. But, luckily, that's not how it works.

Here's my experiment to prove this contention. I went through the house picking up as many different types of texts yesterday as I could find. I wanted to skim the texts and find examples of rule breaking—or we could simply call these flexible sentence strategies—to share with you; to show you how interesting intentional variation can be, how needed, how effective. How common this is in the texts around us. Use good manners when the occasion demands it, but not all occasions do—manners and customs change by time, place, and circumstance (although, too often it seems to be a "school" occasion when you're asked to show you know the rules—a little like having your gloves checked at the entrance to the cotillion, but that doesn't mean the most memorable dance of your life will take place there).

Now, I need to show you those sentence patterns I've found around the house, breaking another essay rule—don't list a whole lot of other peoples' writing. But I'm going to. Sharing what I found, first, in the texts around my house. Then, what I found, in a set of my students' texts from last semester, which I've stored on my back writing room bookcase for just this sort of occasion.

Around the house, I collected a letter from my daughter's middle school principal, popular magazines (*Rolling Stone, Cosmopolitan, Science News, The New Yorker*), a book on computer technology, a detective novel, an ethnography, a book on how to set tile, the local newspaper, a memoir, and an e-mail printout. Easily, in each text, I found authors breaking rules, manipulating expectations of rules, making fun of the rules, or just head down, working, not worrying about the rules. All writers, not just "creative" writers do this, though certainly novelists, poets, and short story writers do it very well, too.

- Here, a middle school principal uses a dash to join two complete sentences and uses a coordinating conjunction, *but*, to start a sentence (bold face is my emphasis or insert, throughout these examples).

   Of course, every day will be different—many challenges and much hard work are ahead. **But**, we believe we have an enthusiastic Raa school community focused on providing the best educational experiences for each student. (Letter, September 7, 1995)

- Here, a *Rolling Stone* reporter uses the same coordinating conjunction, *but*, to start a new paragraph.

   Louise Maffeo glances out the window of an organic-food restaurant in New York's East Village and clasps her hands thoughtfully. A strange smile animates her pale, freckled face. "*Mary Poppins* is a movie that's indicative of my life," says Maffeo. "I'm the good girl. I can't pretend. I'm Betty, not Veronica."

   But Maffeo, who has released her third album, *Bet the Sky*, on K Records, excels in a sneakier sort of subversiveness . . .. (Manning, 38)

- Ah! A sentence without a verb (for a very practical reason—it's the text of a photo caption):

  > First divorced—from each other—cohosts: George Hamilton and Alana Hamilton Stewart [star] on the *George and Alana Show*. "We make a dynamic couple!" he says. (*Cosmopolitan*, 227)

- In this piece of highly conversational prose, the writer wants to create the effect of directly talking with the reader, which leads him into an I/you relationship, slang (*okay, brat*) and rhetorical questions—asking a question "for" the reader that the author immediately answers.

  > *Clueless*: **Okay**, so you feel no pressing need to spend time in the company of a bubbly Beverly Hills **brat** whose main goal in life is to perform physical and psychological makeovers on her high school classmates and teachers. Still, this is one **flick** you can't afford to miss. **Why?** Simply because it's a fresh . . .. (Flatley, 42)

- Although paragraphs are supposed to have a topic sentence, be three to five sentences long, and be about a single idea, the single-sentence in *Science News* magazine seems to function differently. Here a single sentence paragraph acts as a teaser—following the headline and enticing the reader into the "story."

  Quest for Condensate Turns Up Another Find

  > Not long after one group set the theme, another composed a variation.
  > In July, researchers in Colorado reported having observed the elusive state of matter known as the Bose-Einstein condensate in the form of a cloud of ribidium-87 atoms chilled to near absolute zero (SN: 7/15/95, p. 36). Now. . . . (*Science News*, 164)

- There are a lot of rules about sentence length and complexity, but the usual urge is for sentences that are not too long and not too short and not too complex. Clear, concise, coherent. Here's a rule-breaker, labyrinthine sentence, which includes a sentence within a sentence.

  > Gardnar Mulloy, tournament tennis player incarnate at eighty-two —**he is six feet one, thin, and trim, walks with the spectacularly balanced gait of a confident athlete, and has a thick mane of white hair**—came up from his Miami home last week to the US Open to start things off on Opening Day with the traditional hitting, together with Bill Talbert and Frank Parker (still only in their seventies), of tennis balls from the Stadium Court net to the spectators. ("The Talk of the Town," 33)

The labyrinthine sentence, properly handled can be elegantly elaborate. And it sounds quite different from the short, sharp sentences of the detective novel that seems to thrive on what can be damned as "primer prose"— short Subject + Verb + Object sentences. However, this short, hard-hitting sentence remains the building block for creating the terse, self-reliant detective we know and love (and notice another characteristic, the one-sentence paragraph):

> Sayres had gone to Doron White, founding partner, previously my ally, and made his argument: I was doing pro bono work without the firm's consent; Crosetti's controversial politics might offend our corporate clients; and I had again placed the firm under the jeweler's eye of publicity.
>   **Doron had agreed.**
>   **I'd made the firm a lot of money. I'd made the firm famous.** But all it took was one refusal to back down and I was out the door.
>   I'd been forced to choose between what mattered and what looked good. I'd chosen not to become Steven Sayres. (Matera, 8)

And to prove that neither short nor long, simple or complex, can possibly be the rule, sentences can have complicated rhythms and balances, parallel structures, teetering and tottering to create an effect:

> I expected this to be an **easy book** to write. To portray the life story of **one woman—why should that** pose any serious writing problems? I also expected this to be a **short book.** The life story of **one woman— why should that** require a very **long book?**
>   Of course, I ought to have known. Didn't my **comadre** keep telling me I was bringing back a **big book?** "*Se lleva una historia muy grande, comadre,*" she'd say, and she was absolutely right, my **comadre.** This is a **big book.** Everything seems to have found its way into these pages, even the kitchen sink. I'm afraid there's nothing I can do. You don't **choose** to write **the books** you write, any more than you **choose** your mother, your father, your brother, your children, or your **comadre.** (Behar, ix)

* In fact, in many sentences, you find curled up and waiting for you a sense of the persona the author is trying to create. For instance, the repetition, alliteration, word play, punning—self-conscious, high-spirited writing— in this excerpt seem to be part of the act of reviewing—that is, selling— a new novel but also of "selling" the author's view; reading his style helps you know if you're going to like Nick Hornby's first novel:

> Can a man hope to sustain both a record collection and a relationship? Nick Hornby's first novel, "High Fidelity" (Riverhead; $21.95), turns on this **racking** question. The man on the **rack** is Rob Fleming, ex-d.j., college dropout, "Reservoir Dogs" fan, and owner of a failing London record store, who finds himself alone on his thirty-sixth birthday with a "Robocop 2" video and a phone call from his mom. His girlfriend has gone off with the tenant upstairs, and Rob begins to wonder if his **low-fidelity** relationship isn't a casualty of his devotion to **high fidelity.** "What came first," he asks, "the music or the misery?"
>   In the space of two books, Hornby has established himself in England as a **maestro** of the **male** confessional. His first, the autobiographical "Fever Pitch," took readers on an uproarious journey through the **mental wasteland** of the sports bore . . . . (Nixon, 91)

* Which doesn't mean that a persona isn't also created in a less rococo text. Here, the conversational, parenthetical, and rhetorical work of this text seems to suit (wears a suit) the interested technologically inclined reader.

> What does Microsoft Windows 95 mean to you as a participant in the PC
> software business?
>
> If you are a software developer or entrepreneur, the brief answer is
> that Windows 95 should make you nervous (**unless you work for
> Microsoft, or have invested in Microsoft stock, or both**). At the very
> least, Windows 95 will change how you sell software and what sort of
> software you develop.
>
> Windows users (**I mean, consumers**) should welcome Windows 95
> as a big improvement over previous versions . . .. (Schulman, 3)

- Sometimes this persona is developed by putting on the cloak of another
  genre as when this tile-setting expert opens his introduction using
  storytelling conventions, transposing them to a work setting in a way that
  actually makes me want to read his primarily how-to book (a tile setter
  with a heart and a good ear for language, I'm doubly interested as someone needing to set tile but wanting to do it with style).

> **Over 20 years ago**, unable to find any certified training in tile setting
> and confused by conflicting information, **I set out to find** the best way
> to install ceramic tiles. **Since boyhood**, I had been attracted to the beauty
> of tiles, and **as a young man**, I would do whatever was necessary to
> learn the tricks and secrets of installing tile and mosaics over thick slabs
> of mud. No mastic jobs for me! **I wanted sand, cement and tradition**.
> (Byrne, 2)

Now I've wandered from rule-breaking to style-making and no one
but the author of these excerpts can tell me if the sentence moves I found
and admired were *intentional*—but by studying them, I can steal them and
make my sentences more supple, more responsive to my writing desires.
Three last examples—a newspaper writer using the coordinating conjunction **but** to pivot the second half of two paragraphs in a row (is it time to
change the handbook rule on coordinating conjunctions yet?); a memoir
writer using the staccato fragment, list-like, to make a point within a very
conventional, well-mannered (look at the use of *whom*) paragraph; and an
e-mail, from an essayist in this book, to me in my editorial capacity, where
alternate typography is used to add levels of meaning to this swift but
affectively flat medium.

> Deputy District Attorney Marcia Clark urged Ito not to proceed along
> those lines. **But** the judge was plainly distressed by the string of recent
> delays that have ground the already sluggish trial to a crawl and have
> imposed new hardships on the idle, long-suffering jury.
>
> He promised prosecutors he would limit the defense to the single
> remaining topic—a pledge that presumably would curtail any last-minute
> effort to put Simpson on the stand. **But** the judge declined to force
> Simpson formally to waive his right to testify, thus at least theoretically
> keeping the option open for the time being. (Newton et al., A:1)

> Of all my mama's nine brothers, it was Uncle Earkie with whom I had
> the most difficult relationship. Not only was he good-looking; he was a

sharp dresser and always had a nice new car. **A Riviera, say, or an Impala. Not a Pontiac or a Chevy or an Oldsmobile, like everybody else.** Earkie had style. (Gates, 59)

Date/Time: Monday, 11 Sept. 1995 16:55:29
To: wbishop@
From: Ostrom@
Subject: on its way

by Federal Express, the **BREAKTHROUGH DRAFT** of "Grammar J."
I **hope/think** you'll be pleased. It finally came together **&** found the appropriate audience, thanks to you and your cadre of readers.

Okay, professional writers in all venues, all genres, play with sentence variation. What happens when you do the same? When I asked my writing students to break rules or to broaden their writing repertoires to include all the interesting variations that professional writers choose to use they were aghast—here they had worked so many years—grade school to college to obey the rules, and I said that wasn't good enough. I primed this discussion by having them read some unconventional writers to begin with: Lorrie Moore in a collection of stories titled *Self-Help* and Terry McMillan in her novel *Waiting to Exhale*, as well as essayists and poets who used alternate sentence strategies. (But, of course, I've gone farther now, arguing that all writers use alternate sentence strategies just as most sonnet writers don't write completely regularly metered sonnets, because they sound clockwork and boring!)

Here are some observations shared in journals. These writers were reading stories, poems, and or a novel in groups and then writing their third class paper on any topic triggered by their discussions.

- Terry McMillan's style of dialog was also new to me. She relies completely on her word choice to convey feeling. Rarely does she write: "'Blah, blah, blah,' she said with verve." She gets verve across in the words somehow. McMillan also uses a lot of profanity, which I am not used to. Profanity was not an option in high school writing. (Rob Adams)
- I'm so used to following the rules, so when I read Lorrie Moore I was shocked. She definitely didn't follow rules. She grew on me, and I decided to challenge myself and tried to write unconventional. To my surprise, this really worked for me. I was actually smiling while I was writing. Usually, I don't like to share my essays, but I wanted everyone to read this one. This essay really taught me that I can still write a good essay without always following all of the rules. (Andree Bacque)
- Since Lorrie Moore's style of writing is so unconventional and different from what we were used to reading, most of the group thought it would be interesting to steal some of her techniques. In the first short story, "How to be an Other Woman" she uses second person. We also liked her repetitiveness. (*Self-Help* reading group)

Like Rob's statement above, this reading group also told me that "my teacher last year would have killed me if I turned in something like this. Sometimes the sentences are incomplete and there aren't real transitions, but we like it." No surprise, then, that these good student, careful rule-learners, were reluctant, at first, to revise away.

For me, this is a matter of coming of age as a writer. I know my student writers are real readers and writers—all the terms, novice and professional, student writer and real writers—are problematic. Like I mentioned earlier, each of us reads and writes our life all day long, every day. I urged them to go ahead. Here are a few simple samples of where they went and where I enjoyed following them as a reader:

- sentence fragment and list to open an essay.

  Parties, girls, guys, beer, no curfew, no parents, and most of all freedom! Yes, these are all wonderful characteristics of college, but along with this new found freedom comes a lot more responsibility and a lot more *stress*. ("Coping with College" by Sarah Minchin)

- a fictional imitation of *Self-Help*, using second person and repetition

  Four years go by and nothing. Then while out with friends one night, finally meet a guy. You like tall, dark and handsome . . . he is tall. After some small talk he gets your phone number and even follows with a call. Give him a chance, you never know what may become of it. What is the worst that can happen? ("Tick-Tock" by Kim Michelle Lapenski)

- an essayist imitation of *Self-Help*, using double-voice (mother's voice and conversational voice of author)

  People will continue to take advantage of you as long as you allow them to; don't forget to take your vitamins; everything you do comes back to you; Sunday mass is imperative; and on and on and on . . . ah, Mom's famous words of wisdom. I hate it when she says these things, and since I've been in college, I don't miss them at all . . . or do I? I swear I'm never going to be like my mother when I grow up. I mean, what does she know anyway?

  She was only high school queen . . . oh, and an honor graduate. Who cares if she had eleven brothers and sister and still managed to go to college. Lots of people do that, right? OK, she's kept her marriage alive for twenty-one years, and I guess I should mention that she raised three children . . . and right now is still raising three more. Maybe she's phenomenal, but I just always thought all mothers were like her. You know, she gets up every morning and has breakfast ready even if it is Pop-Tarts; she always supported my mostly short-term activities (dancing, gymnastics, the clarinet, softball, volleyball, etc.); she would never miss anything that's even slightly important to me; it's all normal mother activities.

  At least this is what I thought until I finally realized that I was totally *WRONG! This is in no way normal!* This is spectacular, amazing, and

now that I think about it, maybe even crazy . . . ("Talking to My Mom"
by Andree Bacque)

- an ironically reported, autobiographical memory using short sentences, for
effect

> Suddenly the flames reached the core. I don't remember if it made a
> sound or not. I do recall a huge ball of fire coming rapidly toward me.
> It hit like a hot wind, almost gently. It kissed us for an instant, then
> vanished. I realized that I couldn't see. We were both screaming. If
> memory serves, I believe I was bemoaning my loss of sight while Kyle
> was yelling for his mother. ("You Look Real Funny Without Eyebrows"
> by Rob Adams)

- imitation of Terry McMillan, using profanity to create authentic character

> She hardly slept a wink. The last time she looked at the clock, it had said
> 5:36. It was after ten when she woke up. She felt exhausted, more so than
> when she had gone to bed. She tried calling him, but got his machine.
> Briefly, she entertained the possibility of leaving a really nasty message,
> but decide to wait. She wanted to bawl his sorry ass out in person. ("Same
> Old, Same Old" by Rob Adams)

- creating a persona through sentence variation—typographical, conversational, dialogue, contemporary allusions, and so on

> I AM OBSESSED WITH INDEPENDENCE!! I know you thought it
> would be more exciting like food, sex, drugs, or my looks, right? Well,
> every story has its beginnings and mine started in the emergency room.
> As a newborn, I mimed to the doctor (because of course I couldn't speak)
> that I would "Slap myself, thank you!" As I grew older I learned not to
> depend on anyone for help. Independence became my guru; it was the
> Susan Powter of "Being Your Own Person." People may argue whether
> or not it's a good trait to possess; I'm just trying to see if it's the root of
> all my problems or the force that enables me to achieve and make my
> dreams reality. ("God Helps Those Who Help Themselves" by Kaywana
> Jemison)

I plan to steal from each of these writers. After reading Sarah, I think about
beginning a paragraph or essay with a list. After reading Kim, I see how second
person works—actually, I've already borrowed some in this essay, talking as I
have to you. Andree's prose reminds me that people have well known ways of
saying things; when I want to characterize someone, I can use their actual words,
or as in Rob's imitation, their speech register. (Remember, high school teachers—like dance teachers and those interested in etiquette—are being asked by
society to help inculcate "good manners." Don't knock good manners, sometimes they're the only thing that get us through difficult situations. Just don't
think the same manners apply to all situations.)

Characterizing someone in a fictional world often turns on creating veri-
similitude and that means having people talk like they really talk. From Rob I

might also steal the nicely balanced sentences in the middle of his paragraph. I could write, then modify. And write again, and modify. Then continue my prose, using, perhaps, some of Kaywana's humorous and effective analogies. For instance, in my advice giving here, am I maybe trying to turn into a writing guru, a supreme coach, a writing star offering you my autograph and ideas?

Well, here I go then, ending my essays with a bit of advice from this expert witness in the sentence.

First, don't worry about anything I've mentioned until you've drafted and explored, finding out what you want to say about your subject. As I said earlier, if you don't know what you're saying, neither can your reader. It's self-indulgent to substitute style for substance, to use rule-breaking to thumb your nose at readers and reasons for writing.

Second, keep a sentence book. Yes, collect favorite sentences everywhere you go—advertising slogans, overheard conversation, your favorite line from a movie or found in a book (even in your repellent textbook on the dullest subject there's probably a sentence doing it's work in a way worth paying attention to). When you read life and/or look at printed texts, think of what you can steal and write it down. Writers save tidbits of thought on napkins, in formal journals, in jot files on the computer disk. You can save sentences.

Third, read sentences out loud. A lot. Read words in lists, signs on streets, phrases on billboards, the strange translated dialogue on subtitled movies, the pompous editorial in the newspaper, the circulars on bulletin boards, and memos in the workplace. Read your favorite novelists and look at how they open or close a chapter. Go to poetry readings and listen to poets deliver their lines, listen to books on tape. Capture the dialogue and accent of individuals you eavesdrop on in coffee shops and wait in line behind for concert tickets. Become a word, sentence, paragraph musician; develop your ear.

Fourth, when you revise, for fun, try out one of your saved sentences—see if it helps you further discover your meaning. Put it in and if it works, keep it. Take it out if it doesn't work. For all this type of play, the computer for composing, of course, is a blessing.

Fifth, you can't get there from here if you don't challenge yourself, take risks, ruin some writing, go to the edge—sometimes past the edge—and back. Finding your way through sentences is a matter of tinkering, playing, working, and then sometimes, retreating. At the same time, there's no dishonor (quite the reverse) in clear, concise, and coherent prose as long as there's also interest there, first for you, second for your reader.

Sixth, what starts as imitation, forced revision, soon becomes internalized skill. The more you play with sentences, the more you know and understand them. That doesn't mean you know how to define predicate adjectives or to list the coordinating conjunctions. It means you know when you're in control and when you're not quite making it (and again, don't leave it up to the reader to decide this—you should decide).

Seventh. Don't be lazy. Play hard. Enjoy.
Eighth: ?

Works Cited

Behar, Ruth. 1993. *Translated Woman: Crossing the Border with Experanza's Story.* Boston, MA: Beacon Press.

Byrne, Michael. 1995. *Setting Tile.* Newton, CT: The Taunton Press.

Cosmopolitan. Photo caption. September 1995: 227.

Flatley, Guy. "Movies" *Cosmopolitan,* September 1995: 42.

Gates, Henry Louis, Jr. 1994. *Colored People: A Memoir.* New York, NY: Knopf, 59.

Letter from Augusta Raa Middle School principal to parents, September 7, 1995.

Matera, Lia. 1994. *Face Value.* New York, NY: Simon and Schuster.

McMillan, Terry. 1993. *Waiting to Exhale.* New York, NY.

Moore, Lorrie. 1985. Self-Help. New York, NY: Plume.

Newton, Jim, Stepanie Simon, and Ian James. "Ito Puts Spurs to Trial" *Tallahassee Democrat* Tuesday, September 12, 1995. A: 1.

Nixon, Rob. "Revolutions Per Minute: Love, Nostalgia, and the Records People Play. *The New Yorker.* September 11, 1995: 91.

Rosenblatt, Louise M. 1983. *Literature as Exploration.* 4th ed. New York, NY: MLA.

Schulman, Andrew. 1994. *Unauthorized Windows 95" A Developer's Guide to Exploring the Foundations of Windows "Chicago."* San Mateo, CA: International Data Group Books Worldwide.

Science News. 148.11 (September 9, 1995): 161–176.

"The Talk of the Town" *The New Yorker.* September 11, 1995: 33.

13

Talk *Is* Writing
Style in Computer-Mediated Discourse

Carrie Leverenz

Like many people, I now do almost all of my writing on a computer, from typing notes or an outline, to composing a first draft, to revising, to running the spell-checker before I print out the final copy. For me, computers make writing essays easier: I can type my thoughts faster than I can write them with a pen and paper, and my hands don't get as tired; I can add and delete and move sentences and paragraphs and pages by pushing a few keys, and I don't have to type the whole thing when I'm done. To be honest, though, the essays I write on the computer aren't much different from the ones I used to handwrite and then type, except that they are usually revised more extensively and are more likely to be turned in on time, since I don't have to stay up all night typing the final draft.

When I started teaching writing in a computer classroom, however, I realized that computers also make it possible to do writing that is very different from a traditional essay. This writing, which might take the form of e-mail messages from one person to another or an on-line conversation in which everyone writes to each other over the computer at the same time, doesn't seem much like a traditional essay, for the reader or the writer. The writing can be disjointed, with some paragraphs only loosely connected to the ones that came before and others going off in completely new directions. Some of the writing is formal, with complete sentences, sophisticated vocabulary, and correct punctuation, and some is informal, full of fragments, misspellings, slang, and colloquial expressions. Here's a portion of an on-line conversation (called "Interchange" on the Daedalus software system we use in my class), that illustrates what I mean. The class was writing (or were they talking?) about how our community memberships affect our language practices and ultimately, our identities.

Scott: My language practices have been influenced by the places I've lived in. Since I have lived overseas and in different cultures it has definately been influenced.

Henry: d.j. whats up doc its ten o'clock.

Aletha: My identity has been shaped by my ethinic background and my religious background.

Jimmy: Llamare, your a punk.

Shonna: Aletha, I think you need to learn Lawrence's phone #.

Kristy: My identity has been shaped by being the first one to go to a major college in my family. I think playing sports has made me work hard in school.

Henry: jimmy, your crazy.

Ricky: My identity has been shaped by going to school and learning reading and writing.

William: In my opinion, I don't think people are effected by a community as much as they would be by one person or a role model.

Jason: Being part of the southern Christian community I found that the church was a perfect place to become a rebel, releasing a large part of my identity.

Aletha: To Henry: I saw your father on Monroe St. riding a skateboard butt naked with a bow tie drinking a Yoo-hoo.

Henry: guess who coming for dinner the funky dread locs.

Christie: My identity has been influenced by the many different communities that I have been to in my life. I have lived in many parts of the world, opening my eyes to what other communities are like. I have lived the majority of life in Japan, and that has helped me understand the world's point of view in besides that of the U.S.

William: Let us out of class early !!!!!

Shonna: Dean Jimmy: Call me sometimes. I miss you. -Lysa M.

Joseph: My identity has been strongly influenced by my Cuban culture and my city, Miami. My Cuban culture has influenced my language because I find myself speaking spanglish when I'm talking to friends.

Jimmy: Aletha, you need to take writing more seriously or you will flunk ENC 1101.

Christopher: When do we get out of class?

Jin: Being a member of a concert band in high school really affected my identity.

This on-line conversation might not seem much like what we think of as writing—it's unfocused, disorganized, and mixes all kinds of writing styles. Though some writers are writing about their community memberships (as the teacher asked them to), others are making jokes, asking the teacher questions, inventing imaginary students (Lysa) to participate in the conversation. Ideas are batted around without necessarily being fully explained or developed. These writers aren't worried about supporting a thesis statement or organizing their ideas so they lead to a logical concluding paragraph. And they don't spend much time editing their contributions before they send them, since taking too long to compose a message means the conversation will pass you by.

Writing teachers and researchers who advocate this kind of writing argue that it has several important advantages. First, on-line writing is a good way for writers to try out ideas for assignments and get feedback from others. Second, because this kind of writing is done quickly without editing, it can help writers overcome writer's block and increase their fluency. Third, the fact that this kind of writing usually isn't graded also helps writers write more freely. Perhaps most important, by giving writers a chance to use an informal, more speechlike style, on-line writing can be easier and more fun than traditional essay writing, making even reluctant writers *want* to write. Joseph, a participant in the conversation above, agrees that Interchange allows for a writing style different from that used in traditional school essays.

> The analysis that I have made about the writing style that students use on Interchange is that everyone basically writes the way they talk. It seems that on Interchange they have an opportunity to express their feelings in this manner. There is one point that should be mentioned and that is that everyone has their own way of speaking. It depends on the region in which you are from and that is what dictates the way that you are going to write and speak. Therefore, those students who come from the South will talk on Interchange a little different than some one who is from the North. They will both be able to communicate, obviously, but some of the slang words or colloquialisms will be different. The idea that must be stated is that students definitely don't write on Interchange the same way they write an essay. It's obvious to why the two styles are different. They're different because as students we are taught the "proper" or formal way to write an essay and this format is not the way that most students speak. I think that it should be clear that speaking style and writing style are two different styles. Students know or at least think that if they were to write the way that they spoke they would fail.

I probably don't need to point out that the paragraph I've just quoted came from an essay Joseph wrote, not from an on-line conversation. Joseph's comparison of essay writing and on-line writing is written in a style most readers would describe as formal, school-like writing. Note the long introductory phrases he uses before he makes his point: "The analysis I have made about the writing style students use on Interchange is . . ." or "There is one point that should be mentioned . . . " or "I think that it should be clear that . . .". He also uses words and phrases that he would rarely use when speaking: "It seems that," "Therefore," "It is obvious to why," "in that manner." In contrast, the style he uses when writing on Interchange is more conversational, more like talk: "My identity has been strongly influenced by my Cuban culture and my city, Miami. My Cuban culture has influenced my language because I find myself speaking spanglish when I'm talking to friends." Few unnecessary words. No academic posturing. A fairly straightforward statement. As Joseph unintentionally illustrates, on-line writing is not only more fun than writing formal essays, it can also be an especially effective kind of writing, especially when what is called for is the expression of ideas or opinions in a direct and unembellished style.

Many other writers in my class agreed with Joseph that computer-based conversations allow for an "alternate" style that they characterize as less formal than traditional essays, a style that is closer to talk. During an Interchange conversation about writing on Interchange, Leekemase writes, "I think the difference between the two are that Interchange is informal. It starts off answering a question and ends up nowhere. It really doesn't have any particular style or meaning, but just to answer the question or discuss with other how you feel about what they have to say." Aletha agrees that Interchange allows for a free(er) expression of feeling. Says (or writes?) Aletha, "I don't think that the interchange should be edited and polished because it's just simply writing your feelings and when you write how you feel you shouldn't have to worry about all that, its hard enough trying to find the right words to express exactly how you feel and so you shouldn't have to go back and revise it. How can you revise your feelings??????"

Shonna and Thiondra point out that it is easier for them to express their feelings about a subject if they don't have to contort those feelings into a specific form. According to Shonna, "I think people feel more comfortable writing by Interchange. People may feel more comfortable because there is not a certain way you have to say something." And for Thiondra, "I think essays aren't fun because they are usually assigned by the instructor so the student really doesn't have any input of what they want to write about. In the Interchange you're basically giving your opinion on different subject matters and you don't have to meet certain criteria."

That writing on Interchange allows writers to express themselves honestly and directly is further emphasized by Jimmy, who admits, "For a teacher I feel Interchange conversation is much easier to work with than an essay. The information is brief and to the point. On essay's students tend to write a lot of B.S." That's a pretty direct slam on most school writing, one that might have been harder to express in a formal essay. (Imagine a formal essay about how formal essays are a lot of b.s.!)

Perhaps one reason writers feel comfortable expressing their feelings on

Interchange is because on-line conversations, at least those that take place in most classrooms, are addressed to a real audience, and that differs from the formal writing we do that is addressed to some "general audience" or an audience of faceless "peers." In classrooms, writers may send their remarks to their best friend sitting across the room; or they can use the Internet to send messages to friends living all over the country. Not only do we write to a real, live person or persons, but we expect and usually get a response, sometimes within minutes. These responses, like a voice over the telephone, are our reward for having expressed ourselves, for having shared our feelings and opinions. We say/write something and it affects someone, making us want to do it again.

So far I've been suggesting that computer-based conversations allow a style of writing different from the traditional essay and more like talk. But computer conversations are not exactly like talk, at least not the talk that typically takes place in class. One important difference is that in a classroom Interchange discussion or on a computer bulletin board, everyone talks/writes at the same time, and the computer loads messages as they are sent. As a result, messages appear on the computer screen in a seemingly unrelated order, which can make reading them a little frustrating for those of us used to reading texts written by a single person, who has taken care to organize her ideas in a logical way. Ricky comments, "What the past Interchange is, is just a series of statements that have no real cohesiveness and unity because they are opinions of different people." But because everyone *can* write at the same time, more people are able to participate: They don't have to wait until the big mouth in the front shuts up or until the teacher calls on them. As Christie put it (in an Interchange conversation about Interchange), "Not being a person with a ability to speak in front of an audience—no matter the size—Interchange has given me many opportunities to express myself. . . . I believe I have a better sense of accomplishment whenever the class engages in Interchange discussions. . . . I realize that I really go into depth during the Interchange discussions; I let my emotions run wild on the computer."

More people participating means more ideas get expressed. Unlike most class discussions where students direct their remarks to the teacher, and the teacher comments after each student speaks (making the teacher's voice by far the one most frequently heard) in on-line conversations, students talk to each other as well as to the teacher, and the teacher's "voice" becomes just one among many. People participating in on-line conversations are exposed to a variety of perspectives expressed in different writing styles, and each contributor has the ability to influence the thinking of everyone else who is participating. Christie notes, "The class as a whole tends to be more expressive [on Interchange], with the exception of the slackers, and this leaves me with a better knowledge of the views and opinions of my peers. It also gives me the chance to be more open minded and able to change my opinions. You have to look at matters in many different ways to understand them fully." Ricky agrees, "I think addressing other people's opinion is what you should be expected to do because if you draw off other people's opinion, eventually your opinion will become much stronger." Of course, in order to learn from everyone else's opinions as expressed in an on-line conversation, we have to learn a new way of reading. Instead of reading for thesis statements and supporting evidence, we need to be patient with chaos, make our own connections among disparate opinions and ideas, and perhaps most important, we have to participate in the conversation by questioning and responding to the messages we read on the screen.

In on-line conversations, writing is a social and collaborative act where many writers contribute and ideally learn from the contributions of others. Computer-mediated conversations thus function as more than a high-tech invention activity that helps writers compose a better polished essay. These conversations also represent the kind of knowledge-making that students are supposed to learn to do in college, a kind of knowledge-making that is just as important as what researchers and professional writers do when they write books and articles. In fact, although teachers and other professionals communicate knowledge by writing and reading essays and books, many also talk to each other over the computer via the Internet and thus produce the same kind of disjointed, talk-like writing I've been describing here. When I accepted a position as a Writing Center director and needed to learn more about the job, I joined a professional bulletin board—an on-line conversation where writing center directors from all over the country write to each other about writing center issues. Instead of reading articles and books that represented an individual's ideas about writing centers, I could read 50 to 100 messages a day representing diverse points of view. More importantly, I could participate in an extended conversation—ask questions, try out ideas, and get responses from others who were also interested in writing centers. I learned more and learned it faster than I would have if I had been reading only conventional essays. And I became an active and contributing member of the writing center community almost immediately.

Although the writing we do on-line is often informal and expresses preliminary rather than fully developed ideas, this writing allows us to carry on conversations with peers about important subjects. The kind of back-and-forth exchange that happens in computer-based conversations can result in knowledge that is richer and more complex than that achieved by reading or writing a conventional essay because more people's perspectives are represented.

To illustrate what I mean, here's a small portion of an on-line conversation that occurred when I asked the writers in my class to compare high school education and college education and to tell a story of a time when they resisted what someone was trying to teach them. The entries appear in the order they did on the computer screen.

Anthony: Kristy—I am exactly the opposite from you. I used to resist coaches and do everything my own way when I was younger, and everything turned out fine. but once I got to high school I changed my tune a little bit. I may not like a coach, but I'll listen to him because he may be right, he may have had the same problem at one point or fixed a similar problem for someone else, you never know. If I try what he is trying to teach me, and it doesn't work for me, then I drop it and go back to my own style, where I am most comfortable. You may be suprised at the things you can be taught by your enemies.

Carrie: Latrice—your description of your resistance to geometry class was very insightful. A lot of time we don't do things because we don't want to fail. I resisted geometry, too, because I wan't very good at it and it was easier not to try than to try and then fail.

Jason: Jimmy D—How is college the "real deal" and not your future life?

Carrie: Jimmy—if college is the real deal, do you think everyone should go to college?

Kristy: Scott—I agree that college has more freedom to it. In high school you had classes you needed before graduateion and you had to take them all year. It's more interesting to take different classes each semester.

Henry: I feel you will eventually learn more in college than you would in highschool, because in college you learn the lesson of life as well as an education. What I mean by a lesson in life is that your away from home, and you have take responsibility for your own action, your parents arn't their to wake you up in the morning either and you also have to learn to mange your money, these are just some the lesson in life tha you learn while your in college besides an education.

William: I basically agree with what everyone is saying about question #3. Public education is to get you started while you can better youself by going to college.

Aletha: Thiondra, I agree with you when you say that you had more one on one attention in high school.

Ricky: Ms Leverenz, I do not think everyone should go to college because the material is presented at a very fast rate and I do not think a lot of people can keep up with the coursework becuase of a lack of desire.

This is only a small part of the conversation—a collaboratively authored text—in which eighteen writers expressed their perspectives on the poor state of public high school, on the question of who should go to college, on what college teaches you, on how we learn. Jimmy's idea that high school is merely preparation for college, which he terms the "real deal," is complicated by Ricky's contention that only those who are college material deserve to be in college, which is complicated by Henry's argument that college provides the opportunity to learn more than academic skills. Because so many of these writers refer to their own experiences to support their claims, the conclusions each comes to is informed by an awareness of others' experiences. The knowledge about education the group creates is informed by a wider range of experiences and is thus more complex than knowledge any one of them is likely to create alone.

This Interchange conversation may not look like an academic essay—there are no footnotes, no references to published texts, no attempt to be objective about the issue—but the writers involved in this conversation are doing work that is *as* important, perhaps *more* important, to their development as thoughtful contributors to the academic community and culture at large. They are expressing ideas, sharing them with others, considering multiple points of view. And isn't that what education is for?

Such a claim is easy enough to make based on an Interchange session focused on education. But what about the one focused on community, the one where Aletha depicts Henry's dad "riding on a skateboard butt naked with a bow tie drinking a Yoo-hoo"? Is Interchange still a valuable knowledge-making process when writers joke with each other, ask to be let out of class early, insult each other? Well, maybe not exactly, but if writers are going to be expected to construct knowledge together, they need to get to know each other. On-line writing enables students not just to construct knowledge but to construct writing selves, writing voices, that they then use to provoke a response, to get the conversation going. What Aletha and I and the rest of the class can learn from her joke about Henry's father is something about Aletha as a writer—her creativity, her playfulness. And we learn that creativity and playfulness go a long way in getting a reader's attention.

If on-line conversations have so many benefits, why not eliminate the requirement that students write essays and just do computer writing? When I asked my students that question, they reiterated their enjoyment of Interchange conversations but reminded me that in college and on the job, they would need to know how to write longer, more developed, and better edited texts. In other words, on-line writing allows writers to create one kind of writing self; they will likely need many others. But instead of privileging one kind of writing (self) over another, both kinds of writing (the talk-like writing of computer-mediated conversation and the production of formal essays) could be made more meaningful by bringing the two together, a move that would emphasize the degree to which writing is an ongoing process of knowledge-making—about education or communities or baseball or writing itself. This process includes expressing feelings, making jokes, asking hard questions, challenging people's opinions, learning from others' experiences—as well as the physical act of putting pen to paper or tapping on computer keys. For example, when I wanted students in my first-year writing class to investigate theories of education, I asked them to write an essay, yes, but I also asked them to read and discuss a variety of texts in class, to talk in small groups, to write on-line, to interview students outside of the class, and to include any of the material produced in those contexts in their essays. By including excerpts from this "talk" in their writing, these writers recognized the contributions that others made to their knowledge about education. And it should be obvious that I could not be writing an essay about computer-mediated writing without drawing from the many conversations (both on-line and off) I had with my students about their experiences with Interchange. They helped construct the knowledge about computer writing that I am now sharing with you and that you may be responding to and extending through your own classroom conversation—in class discussion, on-line writing, individual journal entries, and so on.

Even as I write this essay, I wish you could send me a response, tell me which ideas you agree with, which claims you question, share with me your ideas about and experiences with computers and writing, so that my knowledge won't end with what I have written here but will continue to change and grow. I also wouldn't mind hearing (reading?) a few jokes and getting to know the writing self that you construct on-line. While I'm waiting, I'll have to settle for taking this essay into my next writing class, loading it on the computer, and inviting a new group of writers to contribute to the conversation that I have begun here. But as soon as you get on e-mail, I want to hear from you! Send all responses to "cleveren@garnet.acns.fsu.edu".

14

Putting Correctness in Its Place
Justifications for Teaching and Learning Alternate Grammars

Thomas O'Donnell

What profits correctness in speech which is not followed by the listeners when there is no reason for speaking if what is said is not understood by those on whose account we speak?

Saint Augustine, *On Christian Doctrine*

On the down side of being an English teacher is the possibility of being forced into the role of correctness cop when you least expect it. When people ask me what I do, and I say "I'm an English teacher," I now prepare myself for standard, sometimes anxious responses: "OOPS, I'd better watch what I say" or "I'm horrible at English" or "I always end my sentences with a preposition." Maybe folks in other professions have similar problems; perhaps people speaking to dentists feel compelled to say things like, "I *do* floss, you know." I can only deal with my own problems, and these days, I'm experimenting with new responses to typical remarks. When I tell someone I'm an English teacher, and they say "I'd better watch what I say," I ask them if they don't ordinarily watch what they say, and if not, how do they know what they're saying. If someone says, "I'm horrible at English," I usually say, "I understand you perfectly. What more are you hoping for?" If someone says "I always end my sentences with a preposition," I say, "You didn't end *that* sentence with a preposition."

What these responses share (in addition to being a bit smart) is the chance of reminding speakers of English how much they *do* know and how effortlessly and routinely they employ these skills in hundreds of different contexts each day. Before reaching voting age, most users of English know how to report, question, challenge, argue, remind, urge, encourage, predict, promise, deny, refuse, excuse, justify, exemplify, offer reasons, describe, and many, many other things (philosopher J. L. Austin identifies thousands of these "speech acts"). These are invaluable skills that keep us talking to one another, learning from one another, and making sense with one another; more importantly, they are skills that are so naturally improved upon in ordinary conversation that you'd actually have to work at *not* improving.

I don't like being a correctness cop. I'd much rather have those who come to know me as an "English teacher" appreciate my assistance in clarifying and furthering the skills they presently make use of. I have found that becoming more aware of already existing skills (or aware in new ways—sometimes just being able to step back and see what you're doing with words) helps inspire and shape attitudes and orientations that can facilitate the acquisition of *new* skills. In this essay I want to remind student writers and teachers of writing of the vast language skills they presently command and offer reminders as to how these skills were learned. In doing so, I hope to assuage fears that both students and teachers may have about playing with alternate grammars of style—the theme of the essays in this collection.

During our work on this book, Wendy Bishop familiarized a group of new teachers with Winston Weathers' notion of an alternate grammar of style— the use of unconventional devices, which, although not "correct" or "standard," are sometimes useful to writers. Wendy asked these new teachers to read an essay she was writing about putting these practices to work in the writing classroom; she also asked them to devote journal entries to their impressions. Should an alternate grammar be taught? In what ways is it valuable? What reservations come up? Here is a sampling of responses that led me to compose this essay.

> I'm not sure what I think of this whole Grammar B idea. I guess it sounds like fun (for us adult types) but I feel it should have one of those, 'Kids, don't try this at home,' stickers attached to it. Shouldn't they learn the regular way first?

> In a first year writing course it is important that students learn the fundamentals of clear and organized writing before they begin experimenting. I know as a reader I appreciate good, clear writing over something that is jumbled and not specific such as "a list" or crot might appear to me. I think punctuation and grammar have been created to function in society much the same way that we read traffic signs. They help the reader grasp some sort of meaning from the text.

I think that experimentation can only occur when one has mastered the traditional modes of expression because the experimentation is a response to the traditional. While I would encourage students to take such leaps, I would not consider a student who consistently makes mistakes in usage as a form of free expression. Instead, I think he is just using bad grammar.

If they don't understand the traditional grammar, I think I have to be careful not to confuse them with the alternative.

My main point of contention is that one has to know the rules before one can break them.

. . . we can't neglect to remind them of those dreaded basics.

It's just that I have lingering doubts about teaching Grammar B to students who haven't yet mastered grammar A.

These are legitimate concerns: Committed writing teachers recognize the importance of having students improve their grammar along with other writing skills, and students will certainly face writing and speaking situations in which correct usage is important. I am interested in these apprehensions because of what they assume about how correct grammar is learned and taught. The mistaken notions I want to address are the following:

1. Speakers and writers of English learn correct grammar by being "instructed" or "taught" rules, and correct usage is the result of following rules.

2. There is a specifiable stage of grammatical competence that can meaningfully be called "mastery of the basics."

3. Language learning occurs in discrete stages: You must first learn "basics" or "rules"; then you can move on to other things with language, unconventional things, things that "break the rules."

Assumptions like these are most evident in remarks from teachers like, "Shouldn't they learn the regular way first"; "one has to know the rules before one can break them"; "it is important that students learn the fundamentals of clear and organized grammar before they begin experimenting"; and "experimentation can only occur when one has mastered the traditional modes of expression." The limitations of seeing language learning in terms of learning rules is easily demonstrated: A child of eight can utter virtually limitless grammatically correct sentences without even knowing what a noun or a verb is. If a child says, " I want more milk," and we ask her what rules she is following in composing this sentence, we would probably be greeted with a confused stare. Children, and people generally, learn grammar from those they speak with, those they listen to, those who correct them. In actual practice, speakers and writers rarely, if ever, consult rules in generating correct sentences; confusions emerge from the fact that grammatically correct speech and writing accord with principles that *can be stated as rules*; it is, therefore, assumed that correctness is a matter of following rules. It is not.

The wonderful paradox that linguists, philosophers, and parents all take delight in (in different ways, perhaps) is that children are *so* good at applying the rules of grammar without even knowing that a rule exists; what children need to learn most often are the *exceptions* to rules. When a child says "I goed to the park yesterday," she is applying the rule that pertains to constructing verbs in the past tense, e.g., waited, relaxed, cooked, remembered, arranged, and so on. If this rule had wide applicability, it might be worthwhile to present it to the child in rule form,[1] but there are countless exceptions, e.g., drove, ran, thought, ate, and so on. It is precisely because of the vast body of "exceptions" that it is impossible to specify a "rule" for the correct construction of past tenses. Imagine how such a rule would have to be formulated. **Rule for Constructing Past Tense of Verbs:** "Always add 'ed' to the end of a verb when speaking about the past *except* for the following verbs—drive, swim, drink, sleep, worry, eat, say, speak, read, build . . ."—I can't imagine completing this list. How do children and others learn to construct verbs in the past tense? Case by case, verb by verb: a child says "Daddy, I goed to the park yesterday," and the father says, "No honey! You *went* to the park yesterday." As you can tell, mastery of the conventions of English regarded as "correct" or "standard" take a while— perhaps a lifetime—and depending on whom you're speaking with or writing for, what is considered "correct" may change.

I suspect that the success parents enjoy in teaching language to their children is at least partially due to the fact that they're not thinking about it; they don't worry about errors so much; they naturally ask the child questions and offer corrections in the course of daily living and talking. Teachers of writing, however, tend to pay so much attention to error—students know well that markings on their papers often point to errors. I don't know what my students do in response to these markings, but I suspect that some cringe, some have a beer and file the paper under their bed, some diligently set about trying to get a feel for the error—especially if it's one they're making often. The important thing for all of us to remember is that surrounding the errors are uncountable instances of correct usage. How were these "correct" employments accomplished? Mastery of the conventions of a language, including correct grammar, is the result of millions of discrete instances of hearing a word, hearing a sentence, reading a word, saying a sentence, using a word incorrectly and being corrected, using a verb tense wrong and being righted, and so on—the continuous give and take of words that is best exemplified by quality conversation.

What does all of this have to do with alternate grammars? Well, teachers will feel remiss if they don't alert students to grammar errors, and students may feel cheated if "the old rules" are said to no longer apply. Both teachers and students can take heart! The best way to teach grammar is by doing lots of writing, lots of speaking, lots of listening. Why do English teachers, journalists, and professional writers seem to have such a grasp of standard grammar? It's not because they know more rules; it's because they read and write, read and write, read and write, often soliciting responses from readers time and time again. Perhaps most importantly, experienced writers are writers who have had opportunities to make millions of errors. What students and teachers need to focus their attention on are not rules but habits of conversing and composing—a sharing of the rewards that come from the practices of reading, writing, and speaking in a climate in which doing so feels purposeful. This is a matter of passing on a passion, not a body of principles or a corpus of rules. One of the apprehensions I cited earlier reads as follows: "My main point of contention is that one has to know the rules before they break them." The truth of the matter is that our students don't rely on rules in constructing correct sentences now and they never will; they simply *manifest* these rules when they speak and write in ways that are deemed correct. Trying to teach correct grammar by studying rules is as limited as trying to teach a good backhand by merely *telling* someone how it's done.

Here's a different kind of reservation about teaching alternate grammars. "I think punctuation and grammar have been created to function in society much the same way that we read traffic signs. They help the reader grasp some sort of meaning from the text." Standard grammar does, in fact, function in these ways, but, finally, so do alternate grammars; in fact, that is the sole justification for learning how and when to employ them—writers sometimes want readers to "grasp meanings" that cannot be conveyed by traditional means. If thinking of signs helps, consider a case in which a school of baby seals is crossing a portion of a winding road and motorists need to be alerted—new purposes sometimes require new signs. Winston Weathers puts it this way: alternate styles afford writers with "a much greater opportunity to put into effective language all the things they have to say" (136). In this collection of essays, students and teachers will become familiar with techniques writers sometimes use even though (and perhaps *because*) they violate rules of standard usage: crots, labyrinthine sentences, lists, and others. The point I want to especially emphasize is that these alternatives emerge as attempts to *act* on readers in certain ways—they serve rhetorical ends and purposes. What is equally important is the fact that experimenting with alternate grammars also teaches important aspects of correct usage. Remember, speaking and writing with others is productive because the give and take of words, sentences, arguments, and uses helps *reveal* mistakes.

Teachers can and do treat deviations from standard usage in a variety of ways. A crot, for example, can be treated as a fragment, an ERROR, or in terms of its effects on a reader—creating a sense of alienation, fragmentation, or separation that disrupts the anticipated continuity of a text (Weathers, 137). We can see an elaborate, sparsely punctuated labyrinthine sentence as an impediment to understanding, a testament to a writer's carelessness, *or* as a means of presenting "the complexity, confusion, even sheer talkativeness of modern society" (138). When a writer offers readers a list, it might be a symptom of a writer's laziness, a stubborn refusal to place items in a traditional form, *or* it might be a strategic way to get readers to discover *their own* connections, *their own* associations. If you think of a list in these ways, it can be seen as a full acknowledgment of a reader's skills and resources, a gesture of flattery.

- rule for creating a powerful metaphor
- rule for speaking in a way that establishes trust
- rule for making a spontaneous joke in conversation
- rule for coming up with effective examples
- rule for "politely" criticizing someone

What if my intention in offering this list is to get you thinking, "Wow!" There are so many things I can do with language that I can't formulate rules for." Did I succeed? If you read the list some other way, does that mean I've failed? What is it about a "failed reading" that would make it a failure? I'm not being coy in posing these questions: I hope to be demonstrating the fact that my offering of a list is an indication of my confidence in a reader's ability to follow me, understand me, or even to have a meaningful experience of *mis*understanding my words. Experienced writers know well that the most valuable and interesting meanings readers get from their writing are sometimes remote from their more readily expressed intentions. This is why contemporary theorists who write about language and literature so often point out that using language always involves saying more than you want to say.

What will determine how we receive and treat alternative grammars? That depends. Students and teachers of literature tend to grant literary heroes carte blanche when it comes to unconventional devices ("Oh, James Joyce. Well, that's different"). What I don't like about this way of thinking is that it makes using language in diverse ways, sometimes *necessary* ways, a matter of authority, not purpose. Perhaps what I should express here is my personal repugnance at the thought of saying something like, "Lisa, William Faulkner can use labyrinthine sentences to convey a chaotic wandering of the mind, but you can't— if *you* do it, those sentences are run-ons."

If Lisa has a purpose for breaking with convention, I want to familiarize her with resources, not silence her by invoking rules, but this raises a fundamental question: how is it possible to tell a mistake from a strategy? One teacher put it this way, "While I would encourage students to take such leaps, I would not consider a student who consistently makes mistakes in usage as a form of free expression. Instead, I think he is just using bad grammar." I think this is seeing things too simply. Although we would regard it as a "mistake" if a man in a bar puts a cigarette in his mouth backward and lights the filtered end, it's not so clear that a comedian at *Hut of Laughs* is making a "mistake" when he does the same thing (but the *character* he is portraying is; somehow we know the difference). How do we tell the difference between a labyrinthine sentence and one that is the mere result of careless punctuating? It's easy: give the writer some feedback; report honestly on how her words work on you; ask her what she *intended* to do with her words; find out what works and what doesn't.

To the extent that the teaching of writing is conceived of as helping students achieve purposes and enlarge rhetorical options, teaching alternate grammars teaches important lessons about standard grammar: a student, with time, will come to recognize that there is a difference between a "crot" and a "fragment," between a "labyrinthine sentence" and a run-on. That difference, however, cannot be determined by citing a rule. The only questions that will decide matters concern intention and effect. Readers must read carefully and report honestly about what the stylistic device *does* to them, how it makes them think or feel. Alternate grammars can supply students with ways of making more meanings and different meanings while also providing opportunities for discussing choices and asking important questions about why a certain "correct" usage is regarded as correct in the first place—perhaps a standard usage makes things more clear, avoids confusion or repetition or ambiguity, or perhaps there's no good reason. What is regarded as "correct" is not always regarded as such, because it assists in the making of meaning: Why, after all, is it bad to end a sentence with a preposition when doing so seems so natural and . . . well, called for?[2] Still, because commonly touted virtues of writing *are* (often times) virtues, we need to concern ourselves with standard grammar; because writers sometimes need to express things in other ways, we need alternate grammars as well. Because practicing both facilitates a heightened awareness of intention and implication, experimenting with deviations from the standard for particular purposes can sometimes illuminate why the standard *is* the standard.

The complex reasons "correctness" and rules have been so revered by teachers of writing at various times they are difficult to unravel, but resistance to such narrow emphases has an equally rich history. Saint Augustine, a teacher of rhetoric way back in the 420s, was making points similar to those I'm trying to make:

> Since infants are not taught to speak except by learning the expressions of speakers, why can men not be made eloquent, not by teaching the rules of eloquence, but by having them read and hear the expressions of the eloquent. . . . boys do not need the art of grammar which teaches correct speech if they have the opportunity to grow up and live among men who speak correctly. Without knowing any of the names of errors, they criticize and avoid anything erroneous they hear spoken on the basis of their own habits of speech, just as city dwellers, even if they are illiterate, criticize the speech of rustics. (120)

The ways we speak and write are not reflections of the rules we know but of the ways of speaking and writing typical of the speech communities in which we find ourselves. The learning of new ways of using language does not call for the acquisition of a body of rules or a mastery of "basic" or "primary" skills; what is required is a commitment to reading and writing, talking and listening, generating and responding. I don't find city students criticizing rustics in my writing classes, but there are many instances in which one language user engages with another to discover common ground or to investigate meaningful disagreements. My appeal to child language learning as a source of insight into how to best work on language skills at any age is more than a convenience. Children learn most of their language skills, especially the more important ones, from their parents—a source of trust, *the* source of truth (how can a child know better?). Familial intimacy is not possible even in the best of writing classes, but there is an important way in which students, new teachers, and veteran teachers can all see that the most important kinds of learning that take place in writing classrooms are indicative of the priorities that come naturally to beings with a language. Julia Falk, a specialist in child language learning, notes that

> The normal response of adults to children's speech (and to the speech of other adults) is in terms of meaning and truth, not grammatical correctness. Studies of adult-child interaction demonstrate that under most circumstances an immature grammatical structure, such as *Daddy go Chicago*, will be accepted, conversation will continue, and the adult will not correct the child—provided that the sentence is true. Even the most mature and gramatically perfect sentence, however, such as *Daddy has gone to Chicago*, will be corrected by an adult if, in fact, Daddy has gone to Detroit. (Falk, 442)

The teaching and learning of language skills are best seen as deliberate, uniquely focused versions of what people do all the time when they try to persuade, offer information, describe, inform, make jokes and puns, offer corrections and competing views, and all the other activities we perform with language without giving it much thought. Considering the fact that Augustine had things right 1526 years ago, it is not clear to me why priorities get muddled and run-ons prompt more attention than lines of thinking and attempts at meaning. If I have succeeded in achieving my purposes, it should be clear that because people have such a wide array of intentions and purposes in using words, the "terms of meaning and truth" they feel a need to employ may not be "correct," but they may still be meaningful. All of this is little more than an elaborate way of suggesting that teachers and students alike, even while pursuing correctness, can profit more by following instincts than they can by following rules.

Notes

1. Notice that I say "might be worthwhile." What I mean is that because children clearly learn language primarily by means of mimicry, it is not even clear that infallible rules (if they existed) would help a child speak correctly. That's why it's so much easier for a child to learn a foreign language than it is for an adult: speaking a foreign language as an adult *does*, in fact, require consulting rules (e.g., "now which indirect object pronoun do I use for "La Mesa" and does it go before or after the verb?"). The fact that

rules are needed for adults to learn another language is what makes that foreign language *seem* so foreign in the first place.

2. I can't pass up the opportunity to share a story about ending sentences with a preposition. While traveling on a plane, a friend of mine witnessed a mother get out of her seat, open her overhead compartment, and take out a book. As the woman returned to her seat, her son, upon seeing the book, asked her this inventive question, "Why did you bring that book I didn't want to be read to out of up for?" Now here's a sentence that ends with five prepositions, but the meaning doesn't seem seriously compromised, does it? (My thanks to Dean Newman for this story).

Works Cited

Augustine, Aurelius. 1958. *On Christian Doctrine.* Trans. D. W. Robertson. New York, NY: The Liberal Arts Press.

Falk, Julia S. 1979. "Language Acquisition and the Teaching and Learning of Writing." *College English* 41.4: 436–147.

Weathers, Winston, 1990. "Grammars of Style: New Options in Composition." *Rhetoric and Composition: A Sourcebook for Teachers and Writers.* Ed. Richard Graves. Portsmouth, NH: Boynton-Cook. 133–147.

15

Sympathy for the Devil
Editing Alternate Style

Michael Spooner

Does "anal retentive" take a hyphen?

Anon.

Let me tell you how bad it is. Yesterday, on the listserv of editors that I read, there was a posting that included this thought.

> Style and rules are the basis of editorial craft; the way these are used is the
> basis of the art of editing. <bogren>

It's a bit ambiguous on "craft" and "art"—and defining oneself in rules leaves little room for either one—but I was glad this person gave editors credit for any creativity at all. Still, can it be true? Style and Rules are the basis for what editors do? This implies a very straightlaced view of language change and variety in style. Is this just another crank, I wondered, railing against the use of slang or the creation of new words, the loss of the good old days when only those who could write the language properly were allowed to publish?

Today came seven comments in reply. Good, I thought; someone else is concerned about this. Maybe they'll argue for a more generous stance toward unorthodox discourse, alternate style, or the like. Guess again. They worried only about the first guy's grammar. (Isn't "style and rules" a compound subject, so wouldn't it require "bas*es*" instead of "bas*is*" in the predicate?) I enjoy irony as much as the next person, but this is a little depressing. After all, this is my profession; these are my colleagues totally missing the point: Pharisees squabbling, while Salome murders John.

On the other hand, I love to read the curmudgeon journalists like James Kilpatrick and George Will, who labor so thanklessly on behalf of the bromides of Good Writing: maxims like "avoid passive voice" or "use a topic sentence in every paragraph." I get an uncharitable pleasure out of their posturing, because in my field (English), journalists as a group are sometimes parodied as some of the worst of all criminals against language. They invented the tabloid, after all, not to mention the headline and the sound bite. Once, in college, I heard a student asking in the English office for directions to the Department of Journalism. "Sorry," quipped one of my profs. "You just can't get to Journalism from English."

But what the Good-Style columnists are selling seems harmless, doesn't it? Traditional grammar, accessible structure, directness, and focus. Many of my editor friends would find nothing to criticize in these. The corny old "Five Ws" (who, what, when, where, why) don't seem all that bad as a heuristic for writing students, or even as a thumbnail stylebook for working writers. How can cheap shots at all this be warranted? Well, it depends.

For me, the Good-Style Guys and that comment about Style and Rules as the basis of editing raise a number of alarms. For example, I'm concerned about the condescending attitude they encourage toward writing done in professional registers, where things aren't always direct and accessible (like the writing of scientists, police, medical folks, or lawyers). I'm also worried about the stance toward writers with experimental aims (thank heaven Stein and Gass and others didn't take this kind of advice). And fundamentally, I'm concerned about what a focus on Rules does to the relation between any editor and any author.

Editing and Surgical Intervention

This is an exercise from a popular textbook on technical editing. By any standard, it is a garbled bit of text, though you'll agree it's far from unconventional. How would you edit it?

> It is imperative in such cases that we obtain documentation that either clearly shows that the pathological process worsened, thus expediting the need for surgical intervention or determine if the planned surgery was performed after entering the study simply because the patient was on a waiting list, or although the indication for the surgery may have been clear to the treating physician before the patient entered the study, the patient did not agree to surgery until after starting the study. The latter two examples demonstrate situations that disqualify a case as reportable and if follow-up reveals either of these situations, the report should be a candidate for deletion. (Eisenberg, 145)[1]

I once went through this exercise with some editing students, and they found it very difficult. In fact, some were even indignant about how dense and complex it seemed, as if density and complexity themselves were marks of poor writing. They're not, but I admit that even I wondered about the appropriateness of this dense passage for a student exercise.

In editing the passage, the students felt their primary task was to simplify it. Straighten out those wandering sentences, shorten them, clarify the logic, make it more concise. (Editors always talk about "clarity" and "concision.") Almost no one really understood the passage, but they "edited" anyway.

Some students rewrote the entire passage in language they felt was more accessible—approximately as easy to read as the newspaper.

> We must document every case that shows the process of disease, and show that surgery was necessary.

Some left much of the original language, but shortened all the sentences.

> It is imperative in such cases that we obtain documentation. This should clearly show that that the process worsened.

Some tried to turn it into a list.

> It is imperative that we obtain documentation to show:
> a.   that the pathological process worsened
> b.   that the planned surgery was performed after the study began

Everyone found it frustrating, and no one did a very good job with it.

But the real problem is not within the passage itself; a few tweaks is all it really needs. The problem here—especially for novice editors—is in understanding the context in which this style of writing is acceptable—and how to make it more effective within its own context. Just to be fair, I'll show you what I did with the passage, myself, though I don't claim this is the only way to make it work.

> It is imperative in such cases that we obtain documentation to show clearly that the pathological process worsened during the study, expediting the need for surgical intervention. Otherwise, we must determine whether the planned surgery was performed after entering the study simply because the patient was on a waiting list, or whether—even though the indication for the surgery may have been clear to the treating physician before the patient entered the study—the patient simply did not agree to surgery until after starting the study. The latter two examples demonstrate situations that would disqualify a case as reportable, and if follow-up reveals either of these, the report should be a candidate for deletion.

The reason I like this approach better is that it is closer to the author's original style and tone. My sense of the rhetorical situation here (the author, the audience, the subject matter, the occasion, and/or the relations among them) is that the passage was taken from an in-house memo from one medical researcher to a group of others on a team. In that case, there is no need to simplify the author's grammar or vocabulary—researchers always write this way. We just need to be sure of the meaning.

I don't mean to pick on the students. This was a tough exercise. Through no fault of their own, most of the students simply did not have a feel for this "researcher style" of writing—it was a matter of inexperience. However, unfortunately compounding their inexperience was their belief that an editor's job is to make a text stylistically Correct—in this case, make it conform to a common-sense model of "clarity" and "concision." And, in their hands, even the clarity/concision model was truncated, since the students all favored style choices toward the "Hemingway end" of traditional style. Again, I'm not faulting them; their preferences were valid reflections of their editorial training to that point. But I do mean to illustrate a mistake they made. None of the students asked about audience, and they missed the cues within the document that would have helped them to identify it. Instead, they were content to rewrite the text as if it were actually intended for them as the primary readers. They believed the essence of their job was a sort of editorial surgery; to cut a text down to the one size that fits all. To their own size.

Ask a child from the city whether the language of school will work for "doing the dozens" on the street, or how trash-talking goes down in church. If you're a middle-class American, are you aware that the directness, informality, and openness of your native communication style (the style of the newspaper, the style generally encouraged in American universities, the style I'm using now) is considered immature, even rude, in many cultures? Getting directly to the point is a big deal to Americans, but "indirection" is the way most of the world prefers to communicate (Fox). It is considered more courteous, more refined, and more interesting.

I'm making a simple point: it won't work for editors to enforce one style and one set of rules, because these things change with the context of writing. I don't need to go abroad to illustrate this, either. In college composition programs that have a writing-across-the-curriculum (WAC) dimension, this point is made clear to students early on. The standard for style in the College of Law is different from the standard in the College of Education, and different from what is required in the College of Science. Technical writing is stylistically different from literary writing, which is different from journalism. What you learn in a WAC program is that it is part of your job as a professional-in-training to conquer the standard in your own field. And these examples, different as they are, are all well within orthodox style, when compared to the work of many creative writers—and even certain gifted but loony academics like some in this volume.

However, when editors talk about editing, we tend to assume that there is one Correctness, and that it is fully described in handbooks on Standard English, in style manuals, in authoritative works for writers like *Elements of Style*, and so on. And where a text does not conform to the traditional conventions of style, an editor will normally recommend—you guessed it—surgical intervention.

Barbarians at the Gate

There's a tacit agreement among editors to pick nits wherever they see them. To be fair, it's an editor's practical obligation to see any miscue in grammar or violation of standard style as an attack on the language. An editor—at least to some extent—lives and moves within an enterprise whose essence is defensive and corrective. And "correction," of course, depends on a standard. (Should I have put that comma outside the quotation marks, instead of inside?) Here's another bit I picked up from the net recently.

> WARNING TO ALL EDITORS AND THOSE WHO CARE ABOUT THE LANGUAGE: you may not want to read what follows.   <lovegrove>

Isn't that a silly attitude? Editors think it's their job to care about and protect the language, because they think the language belongs to them. What they really care about is the set of language conventions they learned in school and on the job—the standard, in other words. And since they devote their lives to service of the standard, you can expect them to be defensive when it comes to variation. After all, it's their job to know these things, and if you allow too much messing about with style and rules—departure from the standard, don't you see—well, how will they know what to correct? How will they protect the orthodoxy?

> . . . in an editorial vein, I do know more and better than my authors. . . . Ever notice that "technical editors" are paid more than "technical writers"? <ngrossbl>

> I have no compunction editing the hell out of a [writer's]copy. . . . Copy is always better when I get through with it, but then copy is always better when an editor gets through with it, right?   <dtallman>

In this connection, editors are not alone. We need to understand something about the culture in which they work. In an effort to justify the fact that they make money from the work of others—particularly from writers—publishers long ago settled on the "added value" argument. That is, as a publisher, I take your manuscript, and create from it a physical product—a printed and bound book—that you do not have the resources to create on your own. I also provide marketing and distribution for the book, which you could not do yourself. In short, without the services of a publisher, your manuscript will never reach a public; the value I add is indispensable.

Now. Since there is practically an infinite number of manuscripts available, and since publishers have finite resources, someone has to decide which manuscripts are going to become books and which are not. And guess who gets to decide: the publishers. Especially among scholarly presses, we publishers are fond of seeing our role in terms of "gatekeeping." We have convinced ourselves that an important service we provide the world is to protect the high standards of scholarly publishing by allowing only the best books into print. (Commercial presses have different standards to protect: salability or "what the public wants.") And we have always been able to make this work, because of our unique station at the gateway to print. (With electronic networks and such, the means of publication is now widely available without going through a publisher. It will be interesting to see what happens to publishing, but I can tell you already that publishers are worried about losing control of the gate.)

This guardian-at-the-gate self-concept has deep roots in the traditions and culture of publishing. Editors, of course, work for publishers; therefore, they have a natural stake in preserving this tradition. And because editors work so closely with the texts to be published, they sometimes feel the gatekeeping duty more keenly than anyone.

Sympathy for the Text

H. G. Wells said, "No passion in the world is equal to the passion to alter someone else's draft."

But look at it from the writer's point of view. A friend of mine and I once tried to achieve an eccentric style in something we wrote for an academic audience (Spooner and Yancey). We were aiming for the sound of e-mail, in a sense, so we did it as a dialogue. We also wanted to interrupt ourselves frequently with asides from other writers—just as it happens on e-mail. We wanted it to become a conversation among many. Nice idea, but how do you show this on the page? To heighten the sense of many voices talking at once, we used three different typefaces in the article—one for her, one for me, and one for the writers we quoted. Finally, unlike traditional cowritten articles, we disagreed all the way through and ended the piece without coming to a unified conclusion. In effect—though I don't think we did it utterly—we trampled some readers' expectations of things like thesis, unity, and continuity. You may see this kind of thing in other chapters in this volume. In short, we violated the standard, and we did it on purpose. Here's a brief excerpt:

> I don't think we have an argument with each other so much, even though we do have more than a single point of view. But we write in different voices, and this is a problem if one insists on proper genres. Can't we just call it a text?
>
> What is the difference between an article and an essay? A dialogue and a paper? Between hard copy and e-mail? Between what we are submitting and what certain readers expect? Those questions

One thing we do agree about is that e-mail offers new ways of representing intellectual life. This is one way.

all center on genre—a central thread woven here. The essay genre becomes a place where genre itself is the topic of inquiry, even of dispute.

> :) This post has been smiley-captioned for the irony-impaired. :)
  <skeevers>

The Digitized Word

E-mail is a floating signifier of the worst sort—whether it's called E-discourse, or VAX conferences, or whatever. So the first task is to narrow the focus. Let's look at these few dimensions . . .

This isn't too wild, but it is an example of what Weathers calls "double-voice" writing (1978). It asks you to read two or three voices at once, and these voices do not agree with each other. The result is a battle for the reader's attention—both visually and rhetorically—which makes the reader feel like a referee. And behind it all, of course, is what you might call the meta-argument: the authors want you to let go of your bias toward conventional "unity" in writing. (Why? is not the point here, but I can imagine several good reasons.)

For an editor who has no experience with—or sympathy for—alternate styles of writing like this example, they can be a real annoyance. And it's not just the funny margins and different typefaces. Good writing, we are taught here in America, has a unified purpose and a single voice. It is communicated in a straightforward argument, with a linear syllogistic progression from beginning to end. These things go to the heart of clarity and concision, which are, after all, the heart of American communication.

But look. If human communication were as straightforward as telecommunication, things would be different. That is, when it comes to the electronic transfer of data, it is very easy to see that inflexible rules are an advantage; machines—even the fanciest computers—are excruciatingly literal-minded. This means they cannot make any mistakes of judgment: Like good soldiers, they only follow orders. That's why the nerd theorem "garbage in, garbage out" makes sense, and it's also why the corollary of this theorem must make sense, too: "garbage out, garbage in." When an error is output from the transfer of data, it makes sense to look for a flaw in the input. There's no misunderstanding in the mind of the machine, and no magic to it, in spite of how it seems sometimes.

Human communication, however, depends a great deal on judgment—specifically on understanding—not just on mechanics; it involves an attempt to match the meanings in my head with the meanings in your head. Since meanings are infinitely idiosyncratic, there are infinite opportunities for you to misunderstand me. Therefore, when we have a misunderstanding (aside from me deceiving you), it is not because I'm talking garbage, but because what I'm able to say doesn't match what you're able to hear.

If an editor operates from the information transfer model, then the common sense idea that meanings are fixed and consistent will work, and it makes sense to correct the text until it conforms to the Standard for style, voice, grammar, mechanics, and the other conventions of "clarity and concision." The trouble with this is that it doesn't always match what the writer wanted to say. So, an editor might change "surgical intervention" in the text above to plain old "surgery," and think a blow has been struck for clarity and concision. Unfortunately, in a text like that, journalist English won't work. You can't just say that "surgical intervention" is wordy, and change it. The writer used that phrase because the nuance of intervening in a process was important to the way she or he thought about the research being conducted. The word "surgery" doesn't carry the same nuance at all.

By the same token, an editor would often be wrong to "simplify" the language of a legal brief or contract, written by a professional in that field. Such documents are quite often dense, redundant, and semantically convoluted; as a genre, they're often the objects of ridicule. However, when it comes to editing any particular legal document, we may only assume that it has been carefully conceived in light of important judicial precedents, and that to edit it by a commonsense standard of clarity and concision might well eliminate some legally crucial elements. We need to work carefully within in the plane of legal writing, and that means first of all that we need to know what is conventional there.

Finally, when it comes to a work written in a radical style, it is a mistake for the editor to intervene with surgery or to beat back that devil from the gate. The style of a work carries an important dimension of the meaning, and a hasty or inflexible editor risks damaging the effectiveness of the piece as a whole. Very likely, the author chose the alternate style as a way to loosen readers from the conventions that editors are trained to enforce.

Common sense isn't good enough; we need a more specific kind of sense. A valid edit, like any valid response to writing, is one that begins from an impulse of sympathy for the text—not from one of correction. What I'm advocating, then, is essentially an ethics of editing—or you could even say of reading— that asks the editor/reader to engage the text first of all on its own terms, and then commits them to helping the text become more effective—again, on its own terms. And this requires the editor/reader to understand the writerly context in which the text is composed and the stylistic conventions that are considered acceptable within that context. It may even mean treating as acceptable many sins against convention, where they contribute to the writer's evident purpose. Editors need a flexible repertoire approach to responding to texts, not unlike Weathers' approach to creating texts. If style for an author is "the choosing between alternatives," then editing for style is, more than anything else, honoring the author's choice.

Developing the Editorial Eye

An editor is just a reader who has been asked for help before publication. Peers can be editors, tutors can be editors, teachers can be editors. Whenever we respond to the writing of someone else before it is in final form, we're functioning as an editor. Because so often in college we find ourselves serving as someone's editor, some of the most convenient places to develop a working ethics of editing ought to be the various sites of the college writing program where writers frequently read, respond to, and edit each other's work: the writing classroom, the writing center or lab, the editing classroom, the WAC program, and so forth. A sympathy for the text presupposes a transactional approach, so it should be most comfortable in workshop-oriented situations, where writers are free to comment on their own intentions, where others are free to elicit those intentions and to comment on the effectiveness of the writer's many choices. Peer-to-peer situations, small group work, collaborative projects all offer frequent opportunities to develop the sympathetic editorial eye and hand. But in any editing or responding situation, we need to keep certain basic orientations in mind. These are obvious, I suppose, but they are worth mentioning.

1. We need to be clear on *who the audience is*. Normally, this is quickly established, but it's important not to make easy assumptions. And one assumption we need to clear away is that the audience is us or someone just like us. An effective editor is one who understands that nothing is ever written for the editor, and who has therefore developed a repertoire of reading personae that they can inhabit as the occasion demands.

    By "who the audience is," I mean a fairly rich description, too—not just, oh, the prof in my business class. The prof as him/herself? Or is it the prof, adopting the stance of a fictional personnel director at a fictional business you're pretending to apply to, for a job? Sometimes the audience is quite narrow, as in the example about surgery above. From the writer's use of "we" and other clues, it's clear that the audience for that piece is a small group, perhaps only one or two readers, and they're involved with the writer in a research project. Sometimes the audience is quite broad, and we need to know that, too. How would you edit my writing here, if you knew it was intended—in the words of Wendy Bishop when she assigned it to me—for an audience of "student writers with ghost teachers . . ." "Ghost" audience of teachers is quite a provocative description, when you think about it. It puts the student in the foreground, but it gives the teacher-reader an important presence, too, haunting the use that the student will make of the piece. How would you help me reach that "ghost" audience?

2. Knowing the audience will tell us *which stylistic conventions the audience expects*. I would wager that the business-prof-as-fictional-personnel-director is more conservative an audience than a real personnel director. Therefore,

I'd think a quite conservative, formal style of business letter would be what the prof is after, to show that we're thinking of IBM and not some freelance software developer in Scuffknuckle, Montana. What does knowing the audience tell us about the medical research memo? It tells us syntactical density and complexity are just fine; focus on meaning. What about editing this paper for students and "ghost" teachers? Well, it's a problem. If you edit me strictly for the student audience, you may make me useless to the teacher. If you pitch it to the teacher, the students will skip it altogether. I'd suggest a direct, linear, friendly style—on the theory that a student will have little patience for fun and games in a piece like this—but allow a few jump-cuts and minor stylistic jokes to amuse the teacher.

3. Knowing what the audience can handle will tell us *whether the author's stylistic choices are likely to be effective*. As the editor's repertoire grows, their instincts in this regard become more accurate. But even the most experienced editors resort regularly to the author for guidance. This is why a classroom setting is so convenient for developing editorial instincts: easy access to the author.

    A sympathy for the text would require that editorial remarks are first of all supportive, and that suggestions for change are going to take the form of a question more often than not. "I like the friendly tone you're using here. I'm wondering, though, if you think Professor Markup as an audience will be more conservative than a real personnel director? Should you be a little more formal in the first paragraph?" If I had access to the writer of the medical study memo above, I'd probably say something like "Am I right that what would disqualify a case for the study is the fact that the need for surgery was already apparent when the study began? So one importance of the documentation is in showing just when it became apparent—before or after the study started? This was a little difficult for me to sort out; what would you think about recasting some of that middle sentence, just to give this criterion more prominence?" Finally, a good editorial question to ask me about this article would be "I'm wondering why you decided not to put this in a rad style. The topic is slightly controversial, and it might help to make your point, don't you think, to cast it in a controversial style? Have you considered using crots, or maybe double-voicing it? What do you think the audience would make of that?"

    Writers are bound to be defensive; that's why the sympathetic question is a stock editorial technique. But don't get the idea that I think editors should never directly advocate changes in the text. I do think they should; I just don't think they need encouragement from me.

An ethics of editing, then, is largely a matter of allowing the author to own the text. It is enhanced when the editor develops a friendship with the writer—and the trust that friendship entails. It requires an editor to detach from the rule-bound gatekeeper mentality and to imagine the text as the author sees it. The editor's function is to make a repertoire of knowledge available to the author—knowledge of language, of audience, of voice, and of style. When advising an author on editorial matters, the editor should encourage choices that are consistent with the author's voice and vision for the text, not simply enforce traditional rules. Fundamentally, it asks an editor to give up childish claims to moral or professional superiority and to redefine editing as a collaborative and consultant activity. We need to understand that sometimes we can best serve the language by detaching a bit from the defensiveness of orthodoxy; sometimes we need to show some sympathy for the devil.

Note

Eisenberg's original includes one or two (intentional) errors of punctuation, which I have eliminated on the theory that they would only distract us in this discussion.

Works Cited

<bogren>. 2 Mar 1995. "plural vs singular". Copyediting Discussion List [online]. Available email: COPYEDITING-L <LISTSERV@CORNELL.EDU>.

<dtallman>. 5 Oct 1995. " ". Copyediting Discussion List [online]. Available email: COPYEDITING-L <LISTSERV@CORNELL.EDU>.

Eisenberg, Anne. 1992. *Guide to Technical Editing: Discussion, Dictionary, and Exercises*. New York, NY: Oxford University Press.

Fox, Helen. 1994. *Listening to the World: Cultural Issues in Academic Writing*. Urbana, IL: NCTE.

<lovegrove>. 7 Sep 1995. "Web site name". Copyediting Discussion List [online]. Available email: COPYEDITING-L <LISTSERV@CORNELL.EDU>.

<ngrossbl>. 26 Apr 1995. "USAGE: editorial tyranny". Copyediting Discussion List [online]. Available email: COPYEDITING-L <LISTSERV@CORNELL.EDU>.

Spooner, Michael and Yancey. (in press). *Genre and Writing: Issues, Arguments and Alternatives*. Eds. Wendy Bishop and Hans Ostrom. Portsmouth, NH: Boynton/Cook Heinemann.

Strunk, William and E.B. White. 1979. *Elements of Style*. 3rd ed. New York, NY: Macmillan.

Weathers, Winston. 1984. "Grammars of Style." Ed. Richard L. Graves. *Rhetoric and Composition: A Sourcebook for Teachers and Writers,* New Edition. Upper Montclair, NJ: Boynton/Cook.

Weathers, Winston and Otis Winchester. 1978. *The New Strategy of Style,* 2nd ed. New York, NY: McGraw-Hill.

Appendix
Teaching and Learning Ideas

Teaching and Learning Ideas

Final Thoughts on "Would You Like Fries with That?"
Darrell Fike and Devan Cook

What underlies "fries," apart from potatoes and the pervasive sameness of fast-food culture, is the idea that form and content are not different but instead inextricably linked. Generic writing, i.e., "Everything is the same," will mean that everything *is* the same: boxed in paragraphs, wrapped up, tied-down, portable prose. In our classes, though, we do not expect everything—or every-body—to be the same, nor is sameness what we desire. In fact, part of our pedagogical practice is in developing rhetorical awareness as we construct, explore, and articulate differences. So we use this essay to teach writing in a world where form and content are points on a continuum rather than opposites, and people and cultures are different. For us, asking students to become aware of rhetorical situations means that we ask them to look for examples of these writing styles as they read and to teach what they've learned about alternate styles to other students (as group projects). It also means that they are aware that in our classes, we want them to try something new, because we think it will expand their thinking and writing skills, their awareness of themselves as writers with a variety of writerly "moves" or "recipes."

Articulating differences requires thinking and writing and thinking again: It means taking second and third looks: It means revision. A student who has learned the "rules" of school writing and turns in a five-paragraph theme of value comparable to a fast-food meal's nutritional profile—basically sound but overloaded with some dangerous fats and sodium—can benefit from some strategies in "Fries." She might

1. Reconstruct her essay using crots instead of paragraphs, going for the "meat" and dropping the "filler." We ask our students to highlight the most interesting or valuable part of each paragraph and to rewrite those chunks of text as places to begin (and sometimes end) crots.

2. Create lists that rely mostly on concrete specifics and details rather than on commentary. She can position those lists to comment on each other. This forces students whose writing is filled with abstractions and generalities to instead focus on things. At the same time, she is considering ways she might connect those things in new ways by simply placing them somewhere different on the page.

3. Stretch some sentences out and break others up for emphasis—explore the plasticity and rhythms of English and what, in context, they convey. Labyrinthine sentences demonstrate as well as discuss convoluted, involved ideas or actions: Fragments bring the reader up short, ask for breath and attention.

4. Use "found text," poems, photos, pieces of earlier writing, etc. to create a collage essay or project, much as Elizabeth Rankin's student did (see "Mumbo Jumbo"), and experiment with meaning-making juxtapositions.

5. Play with repetition, which many students believe to be only slightly less dangerous than arsenic. Repeating a key phrase, theme, or significant detail works as a unifier in alternate grammars—and in most published genres of writing.

6. Create a dialogue with her first piece of writing by talking back to it or writing a metacommentary alongside it. Explore what she really *wanted* to say or *meant* to say. Exposure to and interaction with differences, whether in food or writing or institutions or people, increases students' ability to come up with "the faculty of observing in any given case the available means of persuasion." That's Aristotle's definition of rhetoric. And "imagine, learning something new in English class!"

On Teaching Toward "Risk"
Ronald A. DePeter

A fellow teacher once asked me, "How is it a risk if you're telling them what to do and how to do it?" For example, if I suggest writing the next paper as a dialogue, how is it a risk if the student writes a dialogue? Maybe it isn't a self-initiated risk, but it is a risk because the student probably never tried dialogue before and was never encouraged to put aside the fear of failing at it.

The student samples I used in my chapter came late in the semester, at least half way through. For example, Kate, who wrote the multigenre piece, initially wrote several explorations about her ambitions, a dialogue-only paper on her ambition, a drawing on her ambition, and several freewrites on the topic, all of which led her to some extent to take the kind of chances she did in "Broken Hourglass." The actual assignment she responded to in writing that essay included these suggestions:

You might write your essay in the following format:

1. an exploratory, reflective writing in which you try to figure out what you think about some issue or concern

2. an essay in the form of a detailed letter to a particular person or people (which may be useful for expressing ideas you haven't quite been able to get at otherwise)

3. a scene or collection of scenes using dialogue, description, and inner reflection

4. a combination of the above or some other technique of your own

Kate chose to take up number four.

I don't give this assignment until at least midterm and then only after the student has been practicing certain techniques. Better still, an assignment like this works best if the student has been grappling with a particular issue or topic in a series of exploratory writings or over several drafts.

Crissy wrote "god revised" as her radical revision. That assignment is described elsewhere in this collection, but as I remember it, Crissy went against all the suggestions for radical revision and came up with her own fragmented style. A quality I admire in her piece is the alternate feeling of awe and cynicism; I feel there is substance here beyond the style, and that substance, that willingness to revere and condemn at the same time, is Crissy's biggest risk.

The writers whose work I shared made alternate styles work for them, but some writers in my classes have difficulty investing themselves in such styles. Some students just do not take to double-voice, crots, dialogue, etc. The styles and exercises might best be looked at as tools that may help some writers discover writing personas and voices they hadn't known before, and that may help other writers get at subject matter in a way that is new to them. Whatever the quality of the risk-taking, the risk should be acknowledged.

I think about my peer's comment to me regarding risk quite often. Is it really a risk if the entire class begins writing crots because they "figured out" that I liked a sample essay done in that style? I worry about that, because in my experience, my students will often do anything to get an A in my class; some of them worry more about what to do to get an A than about what to say in their writing. However, I try to spread the risk-taking techniques out smoothly across the semester, all the while emphasizing content over form in hopes that the pursuit of content is not sacrificed for style.

For example I might challenge writers from assignment to assignment to take up some technique. Early on, I will ask them to push for an opening that strays from the conventional. A bit later, I will have everyone write a dialogue paper, suggesting from then on they might consider using the technique. Then, they might do such exercises as lists or stream of consciousness freewrites, techniques that I feel help writers incorporate more internal reflection in their work. Then I may suggest they try an essay in the form of a letter, or a scene that incorporates dialogue and narrative. By introducing the techniques slowly and not expecting finished, polished work each time, students may find some techniques more comfortable or productive, and I provide each writer with a toolbox of techniques.

The Egg Assignment: Readings, Exercises, and a Research Component

Alys Culhane

At the beginning of the semester I put together a course reader. Some of the material was egg-related, and some was not. I selected these particular works because I wanted to show how writers were taking risks, both in terms of form and content. Selected poems included Wallace Steven's "Thirteen Ways of Looking at a Blackbird," William Carlos Williams's "The Sea Elephant," Theodore Roethke's "Dolor," and Adrienne Rich's "The Trees." Selected fiction included Sherwood Anderson's "The Egg," Raymond Carver's "Feathers," and Lorrie Moore's "How to Become a Writer." Selected nonfiction included Page Smith and Charles Daniel's "The Origin of the Chicken," "The Chicken Apothecary," and "The Industrialization of the Chicken." We also read and discussed portions of Gertrude Stein's "Tender Buttons."

Readings which I did not share with my students but which provided a theoretical basis for generation included Peter Elbow's *Writing without Teachers* and *Writing with Power*, Robert Persig's *Zen and The Art of Motorcycle Maintenance*, and Ann E. Berthoff's *Forming/Thinking/Writing: The Composing Imagination*. Readings that informed my thinking in relation to revision included Donald Murray's The *Craft of Revision*, and Richard Hugo's *Triggering Town*.

Exercises

Recognizing that my generation/revision exercise is a bit lengthy, I suggest this shorter version. All exercises can be done collaboratively. Also, other objects can be substituted for an egg. I have divided this exercise into two parts: generation and revision.

Generation

Day one. Out-of-class exercise. Come to class with a list of 50 observations. Be innovative: touch, smell, taste, and listen to your eggs. Responses should be in complete sentences and eggs should not be named. (Personification in early observations limits objectivity.)

> *In-class exercise.* Write about a bad egg, someone you know who is a bad character. For five minutes each.
> Describe what he/she looks like.
> Describe his/her body language.
> Describe what this person does that makes them BAD.
> Write a dialogue in which you "reason" with this character.
> Using these prompts, write an essay, short story, poem or freewrite.

Day two. Out-of-class exercise. Fifty more observations. If stuck, turn to others for suggestions.

> *In-class exercise.* Feature writing. First talk generally about the characteristics of features, then in groups compile lists of National-Inquirer-story headlines. After, choose one from the group selection and write a feature story.

Day three. Out-of-class exercise. Come up with twenty-five puns using egg-related words, e.g., "yoke," "sunnyside up" "fried," "hard boiled."

> *In-class exercise.* Cubing. Five minutes each. Describe, contrast and compare, analyze, associate, apply, argue for or against. Expand upon these in a longer piece.

Day four. Out-of-class exercise. Come to class with a list of twenty-five ways of disposing of your egg.

> *In-class exercise.* Write radio ads in which you sell your egg.

Revision

Day five. Talk about revision using selected readings.
Day six. Journal swap. In groups of two, read one another's journals and collectively make a list of twenty-five triggers and topics.
Day seven. As a class, generate a larger class list on the board or overhead.
Day eight. Come to class with a draft of your poem, short story, essay, or prose poem. (Before workshopping, I generally have students generate workshop questions.)

> Representative questions might be
> What ideas should the writer expand upon?
> What other forms might this piece of writing take? Why?
> At what point does the reader's attention pick up? Why?

You may elect to have one or several workshop sessions. Since so much material usually is generated in such a small amount of time, I choose to have several.

The Egg as a Research Tool:

In this assignment, students interview someone in their area of study about an egg. Such a project (1) acquaints students to the concept of interviewing, (2) further acquaints them with someone in their area of study, and (3) introduces them to the idea that research involves talking to people, as well as looking at documented sources.

Begin by having the class generate a list of possible interviewees. (These can include anyone from any area of study.) Then, after picking three of the best interviewees, come up with a list of five possible questions for each. For example, a biologist might be asked, Why do rotten eggs smell so bad? What, in reproduction is the purpose of the yoke? In terms of its development, what are the difference between a human egg and a chicken egg?

After going over lists and questions, students should first generate their own lists, then run them by their group members. And before going into "the field," have a discussion about the pros and cons of interviewing.

In addition to getting responses to their questions, students can be asked to elicit from the interviewer a list of three possible publications as well as the name, title, publisher, and date of publication. A brief summation of how the article related to the subject of eggs might also be required.

It is possible to have students take this exercise one step further, and do extended I-search or research projects.

Works Cited

Anderson, Sherwood. 1983. "The Egg." *The Teller's Tale.* Schenectady, NY: Union College Press. 134–147.

Berthoff, Ann E. 1978. *Forming/Thinking/Writing: The Composing Imagination.* Rochelle Park, NJ: Hayden.

Carver, Raymond. 1984. "Feathers." *Cathedral.* New York, NY: Knopf. 3–26.

Elbow, Peter. 1981. "The Loop Writing Process." *Writing with Power: Techniques for Mastering the Writing Process.* New York, NY: Oxford. 59–77.

Hugo, Richard. 1979. *The Triggering Town: Lectures and Essays on Poetry and Writing.* New York, NY: Norton.

Moore, Lorrie. 1985. "How to Become a Writer." *Self Help.* New York, NY: Plume. 117–126.

Murray, Donald. 1991. *The Craft of Revision.* Fort Worth, TX: Holt.

Persig, Robert 1980. *Zen and the Art of Motorcycle Maintenance.* New York, NY: Bantam.

Rich, Adrienne. 1975. "Trees." *Poems: Selected and New, 1950–1974.* New York, NY: Norton. 74.

Roethke, Theodore. 1975. "Dolor." *The Collected Poems of Theodore Roethke.* New York, NY: Doubleday. 44.

The Prose Poem: An International Journal. Vol. II. 1993. Providence, RI: Providence College.

Scudder, Samuel. 1983. "Take This Fish and Look at It." *Readings for Writers.* 4th. ed. Ed. Jo Ray McCuen and Anthony C. Winkler. New York, NY: Harcourt. 82–86.

Smith, Page, and Charles Smith. 1975. *The Chicken Book.* Boston, MA: Little Brown.

Stevens, Wallace. 1982. "13 Ways of Looking at a Blackbird." *The Collected Poems.* New York, NY: Vintage. 92–95.

Williams, Carlos William. 1969 "The Sea Elephant." *Selected Poems.* New York, NY: New Directions. 36–38.

Three Questions Concerning Alternative Research

Amy Cashulette Flagg

These three questions inevitably arise when alternative methods of research are suggested. My answers are intended to help other teachers discover their own.

Question: Don't students need to know documentation?

Answer: Most students learn footnotes, endnotes, and text citing in high school. We do use documentation to quote sources and give credit to other writers. However, it is a tool and not the focus or the purpose of doing the project.

Question: When taking other courses how do students know whether to choose conventional or alternative methods?

Answer: We spend time in class talking about research projects students have done in past classes, what expectations went with those assignments, and what the possible purposes teachers may have had for assigning those research papers. We talk about those same issues in the context of our research project. I suggest that whenever students have doubts about what their teachers consider to be reliable sources, and what they will accept in the writing of research, that they should propose what they want to do and why, and see what the professor thinks. Finding out what the teacher sees as the goals of the assignment can help students decide which methods of researching and writing will be appropriate for that assignment.

Question: How do you evaluate unconventional research?

Answer: Pretty much the same way I evaluate other student work. The writings are graded on thoughtfulness in drafting and revision, development of ideas, use of sources within the text, and use of a style and voice that furthers the topic and meets the student's purposes. Consideration is given to writing that was a departure for the student, even if that means the writing does not become as polished in the revision process as a safe writing would have for that student.

Doing Invention for and Writing
the Taboo-Breaking Paper

Nancy Reichert

I have titled this paper the Taboo-Breaking Paper because I ask students to take risks both in content and in form. Because students must somehow *purposefully* work against conventions of style and content within the text of this paper, I find that they actually become more fully aware of the language and conventions that they use both at home and in their writing for class. In other words, the paper helps students to understand language conventions because they must break with them. My second objective is to give students the authority to use language that is comfortable or that is not normally acceptable in an English paper. I introduce the paper through a short excerpt from Michel Foucault's *The Order of Discourse.*

> In a society like ours, the procedures of exclusion are well known. The most obvious and familiar is the prohibition. We know quite well that we do not have the right to say everything, that we cannot speak of just anything in any circumstances whatever, and that not everyone has the right to speak of anything whatever. In the taboo on the object of speech, and the ritual of the circumstances of speech, and the privileged or exclusive right of the speaking subject, we have the play of three types of prohibition which intersect, reinforce, or compensate for each other, forming a complex grid which changes constantly. I will merely note that at the present time the regions where the grid is tightest, where the black squares are most numerous, are those of sexuality and politics; . . . discourse is not simply that which translates struggles or systems of domination, but is the thing for which and by which there is struggle, discourse is the power which is to be seized. (1155)

I ask the students to work in pairs to summarize the excerpt and then to write their summaries in their journals. We share the collaborative writings with the whole class and then begin to create three grids, which help us to understand the excerpt. I pass out three sheets of paper and a crayon to each person, and we begin the vertical side of the first grid with the words sexuality and politics, since Foucault has already addressed these two as being areas that are taboo. I ask students to name other taboo areas, and they normally name religion, homosexuality, and race among other things. The vertical line of the grid is complete. I then ask what types of people they encounter, and they name teachers, parents police officers, same sex friends, opposite-sex friends, friends of different races, and so on. I write these types of people horizontally at the bottom of the grid. I ask them to copy the grid onto a sheet of paper and ask them to begin shading in the grid. I tell them that if they can speak freely of the topic in the situation to leave the square blank. I tell them to shade in from lightest to darkest as they feel themselves growing more powerless to speak freely about the subject in that situation. Once we are done with the first grid, we make two more keeping the vertical row of topics but changing the horizontal bottom row. The second grid varies in the circumstances (classroom, a party, a date, their dorm room, and their parents' homes and so on), and the third grid varies in the type of writing (essay, summary, letter to friend, freewrite, diary, and so on).

Once the three grids are finished, we begin to discuss what they say about our individual freedom and power to speak. I then assign the paper pointing out that if they are to write a paper that will break taboos, they can't write traditional essays because such writings shut down their power to speak freely. I also point out that they need to write on a topic that they normally would not feel open to do so in an English classroom. I end the class by asking them to think of a controversial topic or question for the next class period.

A second invention technique for this paper is called "written conversation." Students bring their controversial topics or questions to class, write them on a blank sheet of paper, and turn them in. I, too, normally share in this activity. Students then form a circle, and I distribute the papers. I tell them to respond to whatever topic or question they receive and that they should attempt to break boundaries in their response. I tell them that we normally write from left to right and that they should do something other than that. As soon as they are finished responding, they are to look for another student who is finished so that they can exchange papers. They do this for at least five or six exchanges. I then collect them, ask them which ones I should read aloud, and share them. As I share them, I usually attempt to tie in what was learned the day before concerning the situations in which we normally feel that we can or cannot speak on the issues about which students wrote. Since cuss words often get used in this exercise, I also like to discuss when we cuss and who can cuss. This normally becomes a gender issue since no "lady" can cuss freely.

I usually conference or full workshop this paper. Ironically, this paper is one in which you want to have more control in the student process. A lot of students will want to write on sex, and this can be very productive if you, the teacher, help them come to an understanding of how circumstance, authority, and the way in which they write the paper play on the issue of sexuality. One student of mine wrote of a situation in which he was bragging to the boys about his sexual exploits. I asked him to complicate this scene by having a good female friend join the conversation. The paper that resulted then ended up confronting the female as person/object situation. I have found that this paper has made me realize what is most taboo for me and that some of the papers have made me uncomfortable for this reason. I have come to realize that this discomfort is productive for me, but it is something you should think about before taking on such a paper. It is also productive to speak with students about the fact that even as boundaries are opened up, some constraints still exist. Such a discussion may help students to understand why societies do need to make certain actions and language taboo and may help you to keep a more honest relationship with students about the ways in which taboos play out in the classroom.

Before students may turn in this paper, they must write a process sheet explaining how their topic is taboo and how their presentation of the topic breaks conventional writing procedures. I also ask their purpose in breaking the conventions. I have had students write raps, poetry, narratives with narrators of the opposite sex than the student writing, and so on. Students have also played with what they capitalize and why and what they punctuate and why.

Two Instances of the Radical Revision Assignment
Kim Haimes Korn and Wendy Bishop
Handout for Kim's Classes

This revision will be what is called a "radical revision" which entails not only an extension and refinement of your ideas, but also a shift in the paper's style, content or format. This radical revision is meant to challenge you by causing you to look at something familiar in a radically different way and to give you a chance to experiment with different types of writing. This radical revision means finding your own area of comfort or routine as a writer and stepping outside of it—this will mean different things for different people.

Even though you shift your approach, I expect you to incorporate what we have come to understand about writing thus far. By that I mean I will be looking for evidence that you are taking up the issues brought up in our class discussions. I will particularly be looking for you to move beyond the surface of your ideas, use purposeful detail, have an awareness of your voice and language, and connect to your ideas through the lens of your own experiences. Consider (but do not feel limited to) the following alteration possibilities:

- Change genres. Rewrite an expository essay as a narrative, a narrative as a dramatic dialogue, a dialogue as a letter (monologue, letter, diary entry, etc.)
- Change of perspective. Add a second point of view—speak with more than one voice. Take a minor character, and write the story from his or her viewpoint. Write from the viewpoint of several characters or voices. Write from a different vantage point.
- Change of voice. Take on another persona or voice in your text different from the original persona. Use a multivoice approach.
- Change in emphasis. Rewrite the paper by making what was a minor point in the earlier paper into a major point. Select an entirely different point or lens by which to tell the story.

The Process of Revision. Your radical revision must be accompanied by a *one* page (single spaced), detailed analysis of the processes you went through writing this paper. As you write, notice the progression of your ideas and the progression of your text. Explore in writing how and why you made the changes you did in your revision. Give a detailed account of how you wrote the paper—the rhetorical decisions you made and why you made them (how did you incorporate the responses from others). This process paper should reveal how and why you altered the text by comparing it to your earlier ideas and draft, what you learned through changing forms or perspective, and how the process challenged you as a writer and thinker.

Handout for Wendy's Classes

Radical Revision—"Essay" 4

1. Choose class Essay 1 or Essay 2 (you may not chose Essay 3, because you just finished writing that essay and you're too probably too close to it, making you reluctant to jump in and play with your text).

2. You will revise this paper in a way that challenges *you* to take risks and try something you've never tried before.

3. The revision can end up less effective than the original (there's no real risk-taking without the possibility of failure).

4. The core of the assignment is your process cover sheet where you recount what you chose to do, why—why is this a risk/challenge for you as a writer, how it worked, and what you learned.

To Radically Revise, try one *or more* of the following:

Voice/Tone Changes?

double-, multiple-, meta-voice, interrupting voice; change from first to third or try second singular or third plural; write as a character, change tone (serious to comic, etc.), change point of view from conventional expectations, use Socratic dialogue, change ethnicity, change perspective, use stream of consciousness, use point of view of something inanimate, use a voice to question authority of the text

Syntax Changes?

alternate sentence length, in planned patterns; sentences in arbitrary lengths (all seven words); use computer spellcheck alternates to distort tone; use spellcheck alternates to insert "nonsense" words; translate into another language (and maybe translate back again), double columns to highlight double-voice

Genre Changes

nonfiction to poem to song to ad campaigns, bumper stickers, fables, letters, sermon, journal, fairy tale, recipe, prayer, cartoon, and nontext genres—dolls, origami, game, . . .

Audience Changes

(sometimes really variations of tone/voice changes?)

change from adult to child to alien, fracture or change tone, try parody, imitation

Time Changes

future (flashforwards, flashbacks), continuous present, parallel times, simultaneity, tell backwards, situate in different era or point of time, change expected climax point of narrative

Typography/Physical Layout

different fonts for speakers or emphasis, one sentence per page, large margins and illuminate, cyber text, lengthen, space differently, shorten/compress

Multimedia/"Art" Piece

performance, play, audio and/or videotape, art installation, sing-along, write on unexpected objects (shirts, shoes, walls), choral performance, mime

push your text, fracture, bend, flip, break conventions to learn about them

For next class—bring both Essay 1 and Essay 2 and a freewrite exploration of what you could do with each one to create a radical revision. Share these with your group and decide where you'll go next.

Responding to, Evaluating, and Grading Alternate Style
Wendy Bishop

Those of us who read literature in graduate school know that Joyce's later work and Stein's work of any period are difficult to read, no matter how rewarding. Experimental writing taxes our reading schemas. Instead of quick reliable matches, "Once upon a time" means relax and listen to the fairy tale unfold, the "Once upon a time" of a Robert Coover short story throws us into a topsy-turvy world of challenging textual stress. When I sat down with my first batch of intentionally assigned radical revisions, I wanted to cry. The first few were exciting AND depressing. One seemed to "work" and the next to "fail miserably" in relation to the one that had just "worked." After I forced myself to read and then reread the revisions, I started to see that, although each was stylistically unique, text strategies could be identified (in fact—it was by reading several classes worth of writing over a few years that I developed my guidelines for attempting radical revisions, shared above). Some students wrote snapshots, others produced textual video clips, others created new amalgams, fragments sewn together into prose crazy quilts. I had to have patience and tenacity as a reader—perhaps more than my students had to have—because I had to set aside my English teacher hyperliteracy and stop judging alternate writing against an implicit canon of genres in my head while I investigated the convention making and breaking they were engaged in.

I'd like to share some responding and evaluating advice for writers and readers that I've collected over time. These should prompt you to develop your own—course specific and assignment specific—variations.

Responding to Alternate Texts

Questions a writer can ask him/herself about alternately styled writings

1. Can I describe why this writing requires this style/format? *(For instance, can I assure a reader that this was an intentional choice not simply an easy way out?)*

2. Are there places in the writing where I covered up, patched, ignored problems I was having understanding my own writing goals or aims? *(Did I find that I couldn't pull my two metaphors together in the middle so I simply left white space hoping no one would notice?)*

3. If I recast this as a traditionally styled writing, what would I lose and what would I gain. *(Was this, perhaps, fun to write alternately—the surprise of drafting this way got me started, but actually the topic would lend itself better to a traditional format in the final draft; or, conversely, would casting this as a regular essay lose the power of talking in my own and my mother's voice—a core issue in the essay being the contrasted yet generational echoes between these two voices?)*

4. In my final draft, am I paying attention to the reader? Have I done everything I can to "teach" the reader how to read my piece while still maintaining the integrity of my writing goals and ideas? *(For instance, sometimes it's okay to just come out and label a piece as exploratory, experimental, collaged, etc. at the beginning and help the reader set his/her reading expectations; alternate and/or experimental doesn't mean "anything goes" it means intentional in a different manner—how can I usefully signal my intentions?)*

Questions a classmate (or teacher) can ask (one-to-one, in peer groups with the writer) about alternately styled writings

1. Can you tell us what effects you were hoping for, where you achieved them and where you think you may have fallen short?

2. What pleases you most and/or worries you most about what you've attempted here?

3. What did you learn while going through the act of drafting this writing in this way; particularly, tell us things that you learned that don't necessarily show up in the finished text.

4. Here's how I read your text. Here's where I had trouble reading your text and why.

5. In this section, did you do _____ on purpose and why?

6. It would help me read (understand, enjoy) your text if you did this _____. How would that affect your goals for creating an alternately styled text?

7. Your text reminds me most of _____ writing. I read it like I read _____.

8. What do you wish you had done (what would you still like to do) to push this text even farther? Why haven't you? How can you?

Grading Alternate Texts with Process Cover Sheets

Use a process cover sheet to ask a writer to tell you about how well he/she has accomplished his/her and class writing goals. These may include learning about drafting through changing a text from one style to another, taking risks, pushing boundaries and borders, attempting difficult tasks according to the writers' own strengths and weaknesses, and so on. I ask the writer to do several things in drafting a process cover sheet, which I characterize as the *story* of the writing of the text. I ask them to cast these as personal letters from the writer to me, the teacher (this could also be cast as a letter to a writing partner, to a response group, or to the writer's own self). Here is a sample.

> *Directions*—Choose six out of eight of the following questions and include your responses in a letter, from you to me, of one to two single-spaced pages; of course, add anything else that you'd like to add to help me understand your writing process.

1. Tell me in some detail about the drafting particulars on this writing—where did it start (ideas to drafts on the page) and where did it go (through how many revisions, taking place where, for how long, under what conditions)?

2. What were your goals for this piece? Where were you challenged? What did you risk in writing the text this way?

3. Who is your ideal reader? What would she/he have to bring to the text to give it a best possible reading?

4. To have this piece published in a journal, magazine, newspaper (choose a particular one to talk about), what would have to change? You may be saying why this piece is perfect for a particular site of publication *or* what you'd do to make it fit better. In either case, go into some detail.

5. If you had three more weeks, what would you work on?

6. According to your own goals for the paper and the class assignment, estimate your success with this text. Be specific, perhaps quote from sections of the text.

7. What did you learn about yourself as a writer and/or writing in general while drafting this piece?

8. You've given this text to a friend. He or she says, I like it but . . . and gives you four ideas for making it stronger and/or more accessible to a general audience. What would those four things be, and how would you feel about doing them. How would each change improve your paper or ruin what you've been attempting?

Grading options.

1. Grade the letter as a traditional persuasive essay for the insights discussed and explored, and don't grade the project beyond done/not done.

2. Grade both the letter and the project as part of an entire course portfolio. This may mean allowing for more experimentation (even individually productive "failure") by evaluating this "slot" in the portfolio as done/not done (in good faith).

3. Grade the text on the basis of traditional criteria—a mixture of assignment goals and teacher's estimate of the degree to which those goals were met, using the process cover sheet to add depth to this subjective evaluation.

4. Grade using a combination of these options.

Grading Alternate Texts as a Class or Small Group

Class members and small groups should outline the challenges of the project before the project begins and then again after drafting—grading could rest on "yes or no" checklists of these qualities, each member responding to and grading the project. Classes read a text for a workshop discussion followed by completing the checklist.

1. explores a genre/style new to this writer

2. writer's choices seem appropriate and/or effective

3. uses language/style in an engaging manner

4. explains learning in a detailed process cover sheet

5. explores topic of _____

6. even though unconventional, grammar, and proofreading choices appear, intentional and under writer's control:

7. success of text

Grading Alternate Texts by Teachers

Teachers will want to choose from the most appropriate procedures listed above in order to encourage exploration and to encourage control.

It's important that a writer stretch, but also that the writer know *how* he/she was stretching and that the writer become more and more *able to articulate what was learned*.

It is essential that writers make "good faith" efforts (and that writers and teachers try to describe what constitutes good faith in this classroom at this time).

Always allow for the inevitable failure that good faith efforts may produce. Obviously, there is learning in the process as well as in the product and writers should have both valued in a classroom.

Teachers should make clear what they are valuing and should offer formative as well as summative response.

- Formative evaluation helps the writer improve along the way through initial discussion of projects, peer and/or teacher conferencing, review of drafts, and so on.
- Summative evaluation lets the writer know what he/she accomplished—a written evaluation and/or a written response and grade on the piece (or on its contribution to a writing portfolio). Summative evaluation can and should also make connections and suggest future directions.

Teaching Alternate Style in First-Year Writing: What Happens When We Go Out on a Limb

Devan Cook

In my fall semester first-year writing class, we have just begun work on a radical revision asssignment (see Kim Haimes Korn and Wendy Bishop). This is a workshop course that starts with a variety of exploratory writings or informal freewrites, about ten or twelve during the first eight weeks of the semester, and then moves into revisions and extensions of three explorations. This format allows us to revise those pieces we like best or are most interested in. Grades/evaluations are based on involved, thoughtful, honest, and self-respecting completion of all assignments, with the emphasis on writing to learn or discover—which can be risky—rather than to reiterate a fixed position or opinion (60%), class participation (20%), and "quality" of writing (20%). At least, that is what the course syllabus says; the fact is that I have never had a student whose writing was thoughtful and honest and who sought to learn something new that was not also "quality" work. Now I am asking students to rewrite one exploration of their choosing in an alternate format—even as a painting, cartoon, photo album, or video. The purpose of the assignment is for them to revisit something they wrote earlier and to take another look, to re-see (re-vise), and to see with different eyes using another genre and the new vision of their now-changed selves.

I have an added agenda, which is that by ten or eleven weeks into the semester I am bored with writing classes as usual and need to recast invention, drafting, and revision in order to feel involved myself. My attention span is, if anything, shorter than my students', and I am continually astonished by their kind acceptance of (if not willingness to engage with), drafting assignments that push me close to the brink when I do them—as I try, and often fail, to do.

To begin, I have assigned them to read and write a short response to a draft copy of the first essay in *Elements of Alternate Style*, which I coauthored with Darrell Fike. Since first-year writers were our target audience, I want to know how well we succeeded.

"Did anyone write their response in alternate style?" I ask. One girl who turned in her reading response early, because she was on her way home for the weekend, played with techniques like crots and listing. She said she had a really good time, and her writing is much longer than it needs to be—750 words instead of 250—and shows involvement.

"I did a little," Damon says. "I wrote a list."

"What do you think about using these techniques to write a revision?"

"Oh, I can do that," Damon responds. "I do this stuff all the time, when I write to my friends." Around the room, heads nod, and I am intrigued because when I write my friends, I write very much as if I am writing an academic essay while wearing a sweatshirt instead of a dress and pumps.

I tell the class, "My friend Nancy (Reichert, who also has an essay in *Elements of Alternate Style*) e-mailed me about a student of hers who said this, 'Writing for school is filling up the page with words. Writing for work is filling in the blanks. Writing that matters is when you write to your friends and tell them what's going on with you.' Does that sound right?" Having taken that "filling up the page with words" fairly hard, I want to know what my students think.

Damon pauses thoughtfully, "Yeah." Once more, other students silently concur.

"So you write in alternate style when the writing matters," I conclude. No one chooses to address this. These are students who are well socialized into academic behavior, and they believe themselves to be edging ever further "out on a limb" as this discussion proceeds. They may suspect they are heading for a fall. Damon, who is famous in class for saying what he thinks to anyone about anything, is the only one willing to engage in this dialogue with me.

"For Monday, find an example of alternate style on a package, CD liner, book jacket, story, poem, whatever. Bring it to class, along with a rewriting of it in traditional style—as if it were a piece of school writing. And write a short exploration in which you consider what changed when you rewrote the piece." Class dismisses on the reminder to think about the rhetorical situations in which Grammar B is appropriate.

Writing That Matters

In first-year writing classrooms such as this one, there is frequently a wide range of reaction to Grammar B techniques, ranging from resistance to disbelief and distrust to involved plunges into the text. Like other contributors to this collection, I am interested in the meaning-making inherent in stylistic choices. I have always wondered, for instance, why I use Grammar B in my poems but less often in academic writing, except as flourishes or quirks by which I hope to remind a reader that my writing persona has a sense of humor and a sense of language and, therefore, merits rapt attention and interest. But for me both academic writing and poetry matter.

I believe writing that students do in first-year classes should matter to them; it should not be simply "filling up the page with words." I also believe that students should be learning and developing rhetorical awareness as well as skills for writers like fluency and techniques, which will make the processes of writing more useful for the varied situations in which they write and will continue to write in the future. They should be connecting and dialoguing with their culture, constructing places for themselves in it and reading its inscriptions on them (in whatever order this occurs). And I want, perhaps most of all, for students to become questioning, responsible, and involved writers and learners, people who are not afraid to say what they think in class or to articulate their resistance. I want them to be able to say, "This still doesn't make sense to me," to argue with me or with the text. Even good students like mine participate passively in writing-class business as usual, "filling up the page with words."

So this weekend I've begun to think that Grammar B should have been the focus of the class from Day 1. It's not optimum to get to "the stuff that matters" eleven weeks into the semester, although I suppose it's better to do that than never get to it at all. It's useful to know, too, that students and I are both feeling somewhat alienated from our own conventional writing processes. For someone who values involved, self-aware writing and writing as a mode of learning, "filling up the page with words" makes a sham of the whole process of classroom writing. This is something I would like to avoid in the future.

I began to plan my *next* class using *Elements of Alternate Style* with the idea that I would keep the basic sequence and structure of the class assignments as well as my usual criteria for grading/evaluating. We will still begin with short exploratory writings (about 500 words each) and proceed to extensions of those at the end of semester. But writing in alternate styles and grammars (the sorts of things that students read and write every day outside the classroom) would be possible options for all explorations rather than only for one extended piece late: that's what would change. Of course, students could do this under the current structure of my classroom, but most of them don't think to do so because they assume such approaches are not acceptable for school writing: lists, repetition, synchronicity, and so on are off limits or out of bounds. In order for students to begin gathering information about different stylistic choices and developing rhetorical awareness of appropriate writing in differing situations and for differing purposes, *Elements of Alternate Style* will provide an admirable text. I intend to do some mixing and matching of essays, tailoring to the class's and to my needs and interests.

Possible Scenarios to Mix and Match

1. What *is* alternate style, anyway?
    -   "Would You Like Fries with That?," Fike and Cook
    -   "Grammar J," Ostrom
    -   "You Want Us to Do WHAT?," Mirtz
    -   "Reading, Stealing, and Writing Like a Writer," Bishop
2. Language Plays
    -   "Would You Like Fries with That?," Fike and Cook
    -   "Thirteen Ways of Looking at an Egg," Culhane
    -   "Stretch a Little and Get Limber," Rogers
    -   "It's Not Just Mumbo Jumbo," Rankin
    -   "Grammar J, as in Jazzing Around," Ostrom
    -   "Reading, Stealing, and Writing Like a Writer," Bishop
3. What my high school teacher said we would do in college was
    -   "The Case for Double-Voiced Discourse," Tobin
    -   "You Want Us to Do WHAT?," Mirtz
    -   "Talk Is Writing," Leverenz
    -   "Putting Correctness in Its Place," O'Donnell
    -   "Sympathy for the Devil," Spooner
4. Generation: finding it and making it up
    -   "Fractured Narratives," DePeter
    -   "Thirteen Ways of Looking at an Egg," Culhane
    -   "Stretch a Little and Get Limber," Rogers
    -   "Claiming the Language," Reichert
    -   "Reading, Stealing, and Writing Like a Writer," Bishop
    -   "Talk Is Writing," Leverenz
5. Revision means to take another look
    -   "Fractured Narratives," DePeter
    -   "Thirteen Ways of Looking at an Egg," Culhane
    -   "The Case for Double-Voiced Discourse," Tobin
    -   "Distorting the Mirror," Haimes-Korn
    -   "Claiming the Language," Reichert
    -   "You Want Us to Do WHAT?," Mirtz
6. New writing strategies for research

- • Why Writers Relish Research," Flagg
- • "It's Not Just Mumbo Jumbo," Rankin

Selections from these lists can be combined to suit differing purposes, agenda, and institutional requirements. I expect my next class to use selections from Lists 1, 2, 5, and 6, and to read regularly from contemporary magazines that often employ alternate styles, like the *New Yorker* or *Sports Illustrated*. We will write imitations, moving the style and format of what we read into discussions of campus life or of our memories, and we will also write about and discuss questions like Who is this written to? for? What is the purpose? What is the effect of its having been written this way? Can it be rewritten another way? What are some of the ways? Can we suggest them to each other? We will write dialogues and metacommentaries to each other's texts and try to answer Peter Elbow and Pat Belanoff's "says" and "does" questions for similar pieces written in different styles. (These responses, most recently discussed in their *A Community of Writers,* ask responders to comment in the margins or on facing pages of a text about what a piece [or a paragraph or even one sentence] says—what its message or main point is—and what it does—how it works in the piece and/or how it affects a reader. Such methods of response develop rhetorical sophistication and encourage students to think about the infrastructures of style and meaning that construct a piece of writing.) We will, in short, write a lot: research papers will become short stories will become fractured or double-voiced narratives. Eggs will play saxophones and dance; unemployed verbs will lurk in the corners of the classroom, waiting to be stolen. In all this I hope we will not often "fill up the page with words" or lose the joy and value that stylistic options bring to the first-year classroom. I think we all want our writing to matter.

Teaching Alternate Style in Advanced Composition: Going Around Other Blocks

Devan Cook

Advanced composition students are usually English majors or people who expect to spend a large portion of their professional lives writing, like lawyers and journalists. They have experience with a wide variety of reading and writing assignments and have usually developed a certain amount of rhetorical awareness about such issues as purpose and audience. In fact, many of them enroll in advanced composition courses to extend their rhetorical repertoire or to play with other writing roles than the ones they think they want to follow: communications majors will try writing like lawyers, for example, and literature majors will become so intrigued by the ways language produces effects that they will take a rhetorical theory course the following semester. These students tend to be more open-minded than first-year writers, to be more willing and even anxious to try new things and involve themselves in recreating assignments to suit their own needs. Perhaps most importantly, they are less likely to believe that the teacher is simply unprepared or a flake when an unexpected writing assignment comes up; by the time students reach advanced composition, they like to think they have "been around the block" a time or two, and on those journeys they have discovered that strange and challenging assignments offer rich rewards. Math, business, and history professors also assign unconventional projects.

Therefore, advanced composition students do not need to be as thoroughly convinced as first-year writers that alternate styles and grammars are not intrinsically harmful—they have learned that what they already know won't hurt them. In my advanced composition classes, my goal is to stand back and allow students to explore alternate styles through writing and reading, listening and talk. Where I teach, advanced composition classes are somewhat smaller than first-year writing (!), so we use a full-class workshop approach with fifteen short exploratory writings or informal freewrites (about 500 words each) during the first eight weeks of the semester and three extensions or revisions of those during the final six weeks. Thus, the way I teach advanced students is not all that different from my approach to first-year writing (see "Teaching Alternate Style in First-Year Writing")—except that it is more writing. Grading and evaluating are also similar, operating on a semi-contractual basis with successful completion of thoughtful, involved pieces of writing in which the writer learns something new counting for sixty percent of the grade, with twenty-five percent for class participation and fifteen percent for "quality" of writing. A student who completes all assignments satisfactorily, contributes regularly and thoughtfully to class discussion, asks questions, and draws out quieter classmates and new ideas earns at least a B.

This semester my students are reading a draft copy of Darrell Fike's and my "Would You Like Fries with That?" to get some idea about what I mean by alternate style and to begin interrogating reasons for using it. We comb through contemporary magazines like *Sports Illustrated* and the *New Yorker*, searching for pieces (including ads, letters, and photo liners) using nontraditional styles, which we wish to analyze and imitate. The next time I teach this class, we'll use several pieces in *Elements of Alternate Style* to help us learn to recognize alternate styles and to inform us as we begin to write. I plan to assign "Reading, Stealing, and Writing Like a Writer" (Bishop) and "Grammar J, As in Jazzing Around" (Ostrom) at the beginning of the class. Both of these essays emphasize the kind of collaboration, intertextual exploration, and play that a small workshop class of advanced writers and readers might employ when they begin consciously looking for, analyzing, reading, and writing in alternate styles; both pieces also provide a push to "try this technique" or "it's okay to have a good time—in fact, it's preferable." Around the fourth or fifth week, we'll read "Sympathy for the Devil" (Spooner) in order to look at our writing from another perspective, the editor's, and enlarge our frames of reference as readers and writers. Later on I require three extended and revised pieces, including one radical revision, and to prepare for that we will read "It's Not Just Mumbo Jumbo" (Rankin) and "Distorting the Mirror" (Haimes Korn), which will give students optional approaches for revision and for presentation of research assignments. If a lot of students in the class are on-line (and more and more of them are), or if the class decides they want to read a computer magazine like *Wired*, we will read "Talk Is Writing" (Leverenz), which addresses writing in cyberspace.

Every day during the first part of the semester each class member brings an exploration or imitation to workshop, using any piece of writing from the magazine we are currently examining that she likes but sticking as closely as possible to the syntax of the piece (Article-noun-preposition-noun-verb. Verb. Article-noun. Etc.) or to the piece's shape and overall format or both. Three class members volunteer to share their explorations with the class to start discussion. This semester pieces that began as imitations of a *Sports Illustrated* article about Cal Ripken retained much of that piece's arrangement and syntax but discussed subjects as different as a roommate, a jazz club in New Orleans, an exceptionally stable boy friend, and a transvestite bar.

Later on, students extend or revise their explorations using a technique that another student tried or start a second exploration if they did not like the way their first one was going. The number of students who can workshop their pieces in each class meeting varies according to its length, but each student should have a chance to workshop at least once in the six weeks remaining. Early in the semester a student asked me if she could workshop a piece she was working on for an entertainment magazine in class. The class talked about it, and we finally agreed that we could use these workshops to work on any piece of writing for any use, period, as long as we discussed our goals and purposes for writing beforehand: a paper due in another class, a newspaper article, a meditation, or a letter to an ex-friend. As these pieces are revised, many of them have begun to incorporate stylistic moves learned from reading and writing Grammar B: a rhythm of longer and shorter sentences or a more conscious use of double-voicing or synchronicity. I have not even suggested to students that they try this; they have begun to, as Wendy Bishop writes, "write like writers" and borrow from each other and from their shorter explorations and imitations. On the last class day we also plan for the following week: what we will read next, and who will be prepared for workshop. Then we write brief memos about how we think the week has gone, what we have learned that we would like to try or what we have tried and liked or disliked or not been sure about—and then we go home.

I like this class a lot. It's how I write with my friends, so it feels comfortable and worthwhile to me. The students seem to like it a lot, too, to be excited about and learn from each other's writing. They aren't a particularly homogeneous group, but they've made a community around, among other things, writing alternate styles. When the semester's over, I'll miss them in a way I won't miss my first-year class, although both groups are full of students of whom I'm fond. And I can't help but wonder whether we all like the class, because we've decided to approach the real rhetorical work cut out for us as writers in the academy as play— or, as Hans Ostrom would say, as *plerk*.